Attack of the Political Cartoonists

Attack of the Political Cartoonists

Insights & Assaults from Today's Editorial Pages

Edited by J.P. Trostle

Foreword by Senator Russ Feingold

Introduction by Lucy Caswell, Curator
Cartoon Research Library, Ohio State University

DORK STORM PRESS

Madison, Wisconsin

For Lisa D.
She would have approved.

This book would not have been possible without the efforts of
John Kovalic, Cullum Rogers, Maura McLaughlin, Wanda Nicholson and Ted Rall.

Special thanks to Mike Ritter, Bruce Plante, Scott Stantis, John Cole, Milt Priggee, Jeff Stahler,
Mike Luckovich, the always-outspoken membership of the AAEC-L, and Bill Hawkins and David Hughey,
the Executive Editor and Publisher, respectively, of The Herald-Sun in Durham, North Carolina,
for their unflagging support of editorial cartooning in both word and practice.

Also, due to her diligence and fascination with the computer keyboard, my cat Daphne assisted
in the design of some of the pages. I leave it up to you, the reader, to determine which ones.

First Printing, July 2004

ATTACK OF THE POLITICAL CARTOONISTS:
Insights and Assaults from Today's Editorial Pages
160 Pages
ISBN 1-930964-47-1

Published by
Dork Storm Press LLC
John Kovalic, Director
Box 45063, Madison, WI 53744
http://www.dorktower.com

Foreword

or, "The Value of Cartoons"

As any elected official knows, political cartoons can be devastatingly funny. If a picture is worth a thousand words, a cartoon can sway at least that many voters.

While news stories can tell us a great deal, a single cartoon can stay with us longer than pages and pages of copy. There's no better way to drive a point home than with the tip of a cartoonist's pen. That may be true in part because political cartoonists are so skilled at capturing and distilling the public mood through the images that they create. The value of cartoons is not simply their ability to amuse the reader, although they can do that very well. They act as a powerful record of how societies view the issues of the day. Political cartoons are historical snapshots that people can see and often still get the joke — even if that joke is more than 100 years old. That resonance is what has made political cartoons a journalistic staple for centuries.

"Attack of the Political Cartoonists" catalogues some of the cartoonists who speak to the issues of our day. We can be sure that a political cartoon has been drawn to convey nearly every point of view, and to help us laugh, whether at public figures, or at the public at large. Political cartoons also help to strengthen politics in the process. Every time a cartoon delivers a stinging truth about how government or policymakers have fallen short, it is also urging us to make it right. We enjoy political cartoons not just for their wit, but also for the way they hold the powerful to account, and the way they never pull a punch.

This book is a fitting tribute to the political cartoon, and to the men and women who make those cartoons such a relevant part of our public debate.

Russ Feingold
United States Senator, Wisconsin

Introduction

or, "A Short History of the American Political Cartoon"

"Only a generation or so ago almost every self-respecting daily newspaper had its own political cartoonist. Usually he was the highest paid member of the editorial staff, and his work was invariably displayed in the most prominent section of the front page. Today few of these papers use such cartoons at all and if they do the panels are likely to be hidden away in the back pages. Even when such offerings appear with any regularity, they are of the 'canned' or syndicated variety."

To paraphrase Mark Twain, the death of American editorial cartooning has been greatly exaggerated. The paragraph above is from an article titled "The Rise and Fall of the Political Cartoon" that was published in the May 29, 1954 issue of *The Saturday Review.* John Stampone and several other editorial cartoonists of the time were so offended by it that they established the Association of American Editorial Cartoonists — and the group continues to flourish today. This volume, profiling 150 cartoonists in the Association, is evidence that the attack cartoonist is alive and thriving.

The able Doctor, or America Swallowing the Bitter Draught.

Venting anger and frustration at the status quo by drawing unflattering pictures is nothing new. In the 1830s the French caricaturist Charles Philipon used a pear to represent King Louis-Philippe in his cartoons. It was easy for his readers to recognize their ruler's paunchy face in the fruit, and they also knew that *poire* (the French word for pear) was slang for fathead, Philipon's not-too-subtle opinion of the king. The pear became such a popular symbol for Louis-Philippe that French censors eventually forbade caricaturists from including any pear-shaped objects in their work.

The roots of the New World's editorial cartoons were, fortunately, in Great Britain where presses were not licensed and caricaturists were not subject to prior censorship. British artists regularly drew caricatures that ridiculed public figures and some of these works made their way across the Atlantic where they were copied by Colonial artists such as Paul Revere (pictured above). The freedom to

The "Brains."

THE BOSS. "Well, what are you going to do about it?"

October 21, 1871

criticize political and social leaders with both words and pictures is a longstanding and cherished American right, one that has been upheld by the Supreme Court in cases such as *Falwell v. Flynt*.

During the early years of the U.S., publishing graphic images was expensive and time consuming. Improvements in printing technology made the profusely illustrated magazines and weekly newspapers of the mid-nineteenth century possible, and several published enormous double-page illustrations about events and people of the time. Editorial cartoons were not a regular feature of American newspapers until after the Civil War, when the *New York Evening Telegram* began to feature one on the front page every Friday. Thomas Nast's attacks on New York City's William M. Tweed in *Harper's Weekly* are the best-known nineteenth century editorial cartoons. His October 21, 1871 caricature of Boss Tweed, "The Brains," (above) has been described by historians Stephen Hess and Milton Kaplan as "the perfect cartoon: the idea is humorous, the drawing is well executed; the message is valid; the symbolism is clear, but not yet a cliché."

Just as editorial cartoonists have always drawn unflattering pictures, the recipients of their venom have always protested and, occasionally, tried to silence them. An anti-cartoon bill was proposed to the New York legislature in 1897 by Thomas Platt, prompting Homer Davenport to compare Platt to Boss Tweed in "They Never Liked Cartoons." In 1902 Charles Nelan drew a series of cartoons in the *Philadelphia North American* depicting Pennsylvania Governor Samuel Pennypacker as a parrot (below). The governor was so offended that he had a bill introduced in the state assembly that made it a crime "for any person . . . to draw [or] publish … any cartoon or caricature or picture portraying, describing, or representing any person either by distortion, innuendo, or otherwise, in the form or likeness of beast, bird, fish, insect or other inhuman animal, thereby tending to expose such per-

THE OLD BIRD KNOWS THE WORTH OF A "PENNY"

son to public hatred, contempt or ridicule." Although several other states also passed anti-cartoon bills, cartoonists and publishers did not comply with them, and all were eventually repealed. Times have changed: contemporary cartoonists are often bewildered when the victim of what they thought was a hard-hitting cartoon requests the drawing so that it can be framed for display on an office wall.

In a democracy, the role of journalists is to inform, persuade and advocate. To inform, to persuade, and to advocate sounds like the job description of an editorial cartoonist. Editorial cartoons are signed statements of the personal opinions of their creators. They are not spot illustrations of the news or funny drawings created to amuse and entertain. Ridicule is a powerful weapon, so editorial cartoons are often humorous — but having a gag is not a requirement for a good editorial cartoon.

The Association of American Editorial Cartoonists is not a guild, fraternal order, or service club. The group is rooted in the shared passion for their calling that motivated the AAEC's founders. Annual meetings of the AAEC are part continuing education and part support group, with the intriguing result that ideological differences are set aside as members talk about the challenge of facing a blank sheet of paper or computer screen every day knowing that a pithy cartoon has to be ready by deadline.

Newspapers print editorial cartoons to encourage readers to think about matters that confront them as they consider candidates, ballot issues, and other public policy concerns. Editorial cartoonist Dave Horsey (above) once said that his job was "to poke people in the eye" with his cartoons, and his metaphor is apt. A good editorial cartoon prompts the reader to respond with either an "ah" of agreement or an "argh" of disgust. The best editorial cartoonists are passionate about their values, study current events thoughtfully, and express their social and political concerns with powerful images that communicate clearly. We should be glad when editorial cartoons poke us. As a result, maybe we will vote, sign a petition, write a letter, or even run for office.

Lucy Shelton Caswell, Professor and Curator
The Ohio State University Cartoon Research Library
Honorary member, Association of American Editorial Cartoonists

IN MEMORIAM: 2001-2003

"Lib And Let Live!"

[Editor's note: An El Dani cartoon from 1971.]

Daniel Aguila (El Dani)

Artist, journalist and cartoonist Dani Aguila was born in 1928 in Manila, in the Philippines, and became a naturalized U.S. citizen in June of 1976.

After getting a BFA in painting from the University of the Philippines in 1952, Aguila studied design and photojournalism on a fellowship to Syracuse University in New York. During that time he met and caricatured a young up-and-coming senator named John F. Kennedy.

Over the next 20 years, Aguila was — among other things — a correspondent and artist for the biweekly *Asian Student.* He was part of a team of journalists who covered the independence of Malaysia in 1963, and spent a week in South Vietnam in 1965 as an artist and photographer for the Philippine newsweekly *Examiner.*

Aguila eventually relocated to Nashville, Tennessee, and worked as an art director in advertising, publishing and public television. He also continued to draw editorial cartoons, with his work appearing in the *Filipino Reporter, Filipino Monitor, Asian Pacific American Times, Pinoy,* and *Nashville City Paper.* Since "retiring," Aguila has continued to provide cartoons to the biweekly *Filipino/Asian Bulletin.*

Aguila's work has been cited by the National Press Club and has received several awards from the Art Directors Club of Nashville, including a Wise Owl of Athena Gold Medal in 1974. From 1975 to 1998 his editorial cartoons appeared on a regular basis in Pelican Publishing's "Best Editorial Cartoons of the Year."

Freedom and liberty are driving themes for Aguila, who survived the Japanese occupation of the Philippines in WWII, and they came together in 1986 when he edited and published a 240-page collection of editorial cartoons about the Statue of Liberty titled "Taking Liberty with The Lady."

"The statue to me is a literal interpretation of the word 'liberty,'" Aguila told a reporter in 1986. "I came from a country that was debauched in the recent elections. The statue is a rallying point to which universal man can look for the hope of a liberal, democratic life."

Dani Aguila lives in Nashville with Norma, his wife of 44 years. They have two daughters, a son, and three grandchildren.

Dani Aguila
danidumuk@yahoo.com

[The ectoplasmic shade of Nixon rises in this 1994 illustration.]

Lalo Alcaraz

Lalo Alcaraz captures the essence of the country's changing cultural and political landscape. He is the creator of the first nationally syndicated politically-themed Latino daily strip, "La Cucaracha," which is distributed by Universal Press Syndicate in over 65 newspapers.

Alcaraz began drawing daily editorial cartoons at San Diego State University's newspaper, *The Daily Aztec,* in 1985. In 1991, Alcaraz earned his master's degree in architecture from the University of California, Berkeley.

Since 1992, he has produced editorial cartoons for *LA Weekly* and also creates editorial cartoons in English and Spanish for Universal Press Syndicate. His work has appeared in *the New York Times, the Village Voice, Los Angeles Times, Variety, Hispanic Magazine, Latina Magazine, La Jornada* in Mexico City, and many other publications. He is also the co-editor of the satirical magazine *POCHO* and illustrated the book "Latino USA: A Cartoon History."

Alcaraz has received four Southern California Journalism Awards for Best Cartoon in Weekly Papers, as well as the Los Angeles Hispanic Public Relations Association's Premio Award for Excellence in Communications, and the Center for the Study of Political Graphics "Art as a Hammer" Award.

He lives in Los Angeles with his public schoolteacher wife and three children.

Lalo Alcaraz
www.lacucaracha.com

CONSUMERISM IS SELF-EXPRESSION FOR THE UNCREATIVE

Kirk Anderson

Kirk Anderson's award-winning cartoons have appeared in *the New York Times*, *the Washington Post, Los Angeles Times, Newsweek, USA Today* and hundreds of other newspapers and magazines throughout the U.S., Britain, Canada, Europe and Japan.

They have prompted stockholder protest of corporate policy, have been debated in newspaper columns and on talk radio, orchestrated into Congressional presentations and classroom lessons, chosen for national exhibitions, and collected in over 150 books.

As the staff cartoonist for the *Pioneer Press* in St. Paul, Minnesota, Anderson afflicted the comfortable and comforted the afflicted from 1995 to 2003. He currently freelances his work, and is distributed by Artizans syndicate.

Kirk Anderson's cartoons have been publicly denounced by a governor, officially condemned by a state university, personally admonished by a U.S. Senator, reviled in print by an archbishop and vilified by police, business leaders, talk radio, the NRA, and others. If there's anyone you'd like to piss off, consider subscribing to Kirk's cartoons today.

He currently lives in St. Paul with his wife Nancy Brewster and two invisible friends, Winky and Mr. Tithers.

Kirk Anderson
2064 James Ave.
St. Paul, MN 55105
651-698-4799
kirk@kirktoons.com
www.kirktoons.com

Nick Anderson

Since joining the *Louisville Courier-Journal* in January 1991, a month after graduating from Ohio State, Nick Anderson's cartoons have been published in *Newsweek, the New York Times, the Washington Post, USA Today* and *the Chicago Tribune.*

Anderson, 36, grew up in Toledo, Ohio. At 15, he started drawing cartoons for his high school newspaper and immediately knew his calling. At Ohio State, Anderson majored in political science and was editorial cartoonist for the university newspaper. In 1989, he won the Charles M. Schulz Award for best college cartoonist in North America.

He interned one summer with the *Courier-Journal,* and after graduation, the newspaper created a position for him as associate editorial cartoonist and illustrator. He was promoted to chief editorial cartoonist in September 1995.

In 1996, he began syndication with the Washington Post Writers Group. He won the John Fischetti award for editorial cartooning in 1999 and the Sigma Delta Chi Mark of Excellence Award in 2001.

In his spare time, he enjoys mountain biking and kayaking. In 1988 he cycled across the country from Oregon to Massachusetts.

He lives in Louisville with his wife Cecilia, and their sons Colton and Travis. His son's names are hidden in all of Anderson's cartoons.

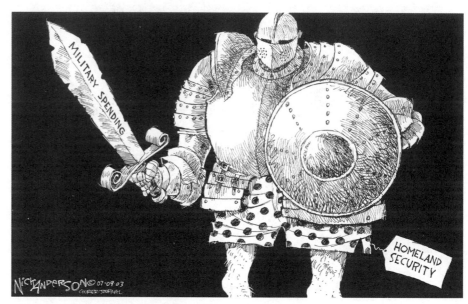

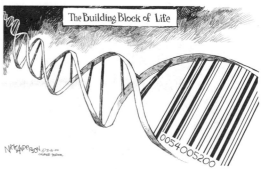

Nick Anderson
525 W. Broadway
Louisville, KY 40204
502-582-7159
nanderson@courier-journal.com
www.courier-journal.com

THE GEORGE W. BUSH MILITARY PAPER DOLL PLAY SET

THE NATIONAL GUARD YEARS

THE PRESIDENTIAL YEARS

Tony Auth

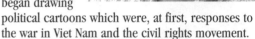

Tony Auth majored in biological illustration at UCLA and graduated in 1965. While working as chief medical illustrator at a large teaching hospital, he began drawing political cartoons which were, at first, responses to the war in Viet Nam and the civil rights movement.

He was hired by *The Philadelphia Inquirer* in 1971, where he has been happily ensconced ever since. Like all working political cartoonists, Tony Auth receives awards and hate mail, and undeserved quantities of both. *[Although it deserves mentioning Auth won the 1976 Pulitzer Prize for Editorial Cartooning.]*

Auth and his wife Eliza live with their two daughters in Wynnewood, Pennsylvania.

DEMOCRACY

BUSH ADMINISTRATION HEADGEAR — AT HOME & ABROAD.

Tony Auth
tauth@phillynews.com

Return to Moon May Be on Agenda

GUANTANAMO II

Rex Babin

Rex Babin got his start as an editorial cartoonist while crawling around on the linoleum floor of his family's Walnut Creek, California, home. There he would crush various Crayola crayons against the kitchen walls, occasionally stuffing a burnt sienna up his nose or dropping a lemon yellow down his diaper. Naturally, he moved with ease to the next medium — finger paints.

Babin has been with *The Sacramento Bee* in California since May 1999. Prior to joining the *Bee*, he was the editorial cartoonist for the *Times Union* in Albany, New York, *the Denver Post* in Colorado, and the *Daily Pilot* in Orange County-Costa Mesa, California

In addition to his work at *The Sacramento Bee*, Babin's cartoons are nationally distributed by North America Syndicate, appearing in over 300 newspapers and magazines including *the New York Times*, *the Washington Post*, *USA Today* and *Newsweek*.

Rex was the winner of the National Press Foundation's 2001 Berryman Award and was a finalist for the 2003 Pulitzer Prize. He was also a finalist in the 1991 Fischetti Editorial Cartoon Competition and the second place winner in 1999. Other awards Babin has received include the Hearst Newspapers Eagle Award for Excellence and numerous California and New York state and regional honors.

Babin received his Bachelor of Arts degree from San Diego State University in 1985. He and his wife Kathleen and son Sebastian live in Sacramento.

Rex Babin
P.O. Box 15997
Sacramento, CA 95852
916-321-1911
rbabin@sacbee.com

Guy Badeaux (Bado)

Born in Montreal in 1949, Guy Badeaux (Bado) has been the editorial cartoonist for *Le Droit* in Ottawa, the capital of Canada, since 1981.

Winner in 1991 of the National Newspaper Award for editorial cartooning — the Canadian equivalent to the Pulitzer Prize — he has been, since 1985, editor of "Portfoolio: The Year's Best Canadian Editorial Cartoons."

An avid blues fan and harmonica player, he surprises even himself by being the treasurer of both the Association of Canadian Editorial Cartoonists as well as of the journalist union in his newspaper. His work is published around the world via Cartoonists & Writers Syndicate and by Artizans in Canada.

Married to Sylvie-Hélène Lapointe since 1997, he keeps up to date with current pop culture thanks to her two teenage daughters, Laure and Gabrielle.

[After a court case seeking equality between sexes, women are now allowed to be bare-breasted in public in Ontario.]

Guy Badeaux
bado@ledroit.com

Bruce Beattie

Bruce Beattie, editorial cartoonist at Florida's *Daytona Beach News-Journal* since 1981, began his cartooning career in college. Upon graduation from the University of Pennsylvania, he continued his studies at the Art Center College of Design in California.

In addition to national syndication with Copley News Service, Beattie's cartoons have been featured in papers such as *the New York Times*, *the San Diego Union* and *Rocky Mountain News*. His work currently appears regularly on *Time* magazine's web site, and has also been featured in several museum exhibits. His work has been recognized throughout the Southeast with awards for excellence in editorial cartooning.

From 1986 to 1998, Beattie's wit was also seen on the comic pages. His internationally syndicated cartoon panel "Beattie Blvd." was nominated for the National Cartoonists Society's "Best Cartoon Panel" Award.

Beattie is past president of the National Cartoonists Society, and has served on the Boards of Directors of the AAEC, the Newspaper Features Council and the International Museum of Cartoon Art. He is featured in the 1995 book "A Career in the Comics" and other cartoon publications.

An avid golfer and flight-sim enthusiast, Beattie enjoys life of the fourth fairway with his wife Karen, a public-school assistant principal.

"The Bush administration doesn't want any media photo coverage of this. How will they stop editorial cartoons about it?"

"It's nice having someplace safe to put up this swing set."

"You be the Palestinians . . . I'll be the Israelis."

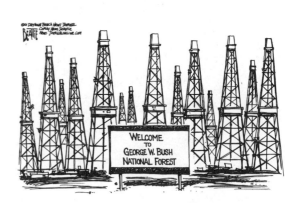

WELCOME TO GEORGE W. BUSH NATIONAL FOREST

Bruce Beattie
636 Pelican Bay Dr.
Daytona Beach, FL 32119
386-252-1511 x2421
bruce.beattie@news-jrnl.com

Clay Bennett

Clay Bennett was born in January 1958, in Clinton, South Carolina. Growing up the son of a career army officer, he led a nomadic life, attending ten different schools before graduating in 1976 from Butler High School in Huntsville, Alabama.

Bennett served as editorial cartoonist for the campus newspaper and managing editor of an alternative student publication while attending the University of North Alabama and graduated in 1980 with degrees in art and history.

Before accepting a cartooning position with the *St. Petersburg Times* in 1981, he worked as a staff artist for both *the Pittsburgh Post-Gazette* and *the Fayetteville Times* in North Carolina.

Fired by the *St. Petersburg Times* in 1994, Bennett spent three years in professional oblivion before being hired as the editorial cartoonist for *The Christian Science Monitor*. During this time he taught himself how to use Photoshop and developed the unique drawing technique he uses today.

Since joining the staff of *The Monitor*, he has received the National Headliner Award in 1999 and 2000, and the John Fischetti Award and the Society of Professional Journalists' Sigma Delta Chi Award in 2001. In 2002 he won the National Cartoonists Society Award for Editorial Cartoons, the Scripps Howard Foundation's National Journalism Award and the Pulitzer Prize for Editorial Cartooning.

Bennett lives in Boston with his wife, *Huntsville Times* cartoonist Cindy Procious, daughter Sarah and sons Matt and Ben.

Clay Bennett
www.claybennett.com

Steve Benson

Steve Benson got his start cartooning at *The Arizona Republic* in Phoenix, Arizona in 1980. In 1990 he moved to *The Morning News Tribune*, in Tacoma, Washington, but stayed only for two years before heading back to *The Arizona Republic*, where he has been ever since.

Benson has won numerous awards for his work, including first place in the Headliner Awards in 1984, the Overseas Press Club of America Citation for Excellence in 1995, and multiple awards from the Arizona Press Club and the Best of the West contest. He has been a Pulitzer Prize finalist on four separate occasions, and won journalism's biggest prize in 1993.

His work has been syndicated by The Washington Post Writers' Group and Tribune Media Services and, since 1994, with United Feature Syndicate. His cartoons have been collected into four volumes. He was also president of the Association of American Editorial Cartoonists in 1999-2000.

Benson received a Bachelor of Arts in political science from Brigham Young University in 1979, and in 1997 he completed his training and became a sworn police officer in the State of Arizona.

He is married to Mary Ann Christensen, with whom he has four children.

Steve Benson
steve.benson@arizonarepublic.com

Randy Bish

Randy Bish has been drawing editorial cartoons at the *Tribune-Review* in

Greensburg, Pennsylvania, since 1985. He produces six political cartoons each week, a sports cartoon on Sundays and many other illustrations. His cartoons also appear on the editorial pages of the *Pittsburgh Tribune-Review*.

Bish's cartoons were syndicated by the Pennsylvania Newspaper Association for over 10 years, and are today distributed by United Media.

His drawings have been published in the annual "Best Editorial Cartoons Of The Year" (one was used on the cover of the book in 1998), along with many other publications. They have also been featured on "Good Morning America" and C-Span, and are currently a regular feature on CNN Headline News. His editorial cartoons appeared in several gallery exhibits across the country. Most recently, they have been a part of two exhibits at the Charles Schulz Museum in California.

Bish's work has been recognized by the Golden Quill Awards. In 2002, he was a winner in the Iranian International Cartoon Contest.

WHY IS IT OUR CHILDREN CAN AFFORD THE DRUGS SOLD ON THE STREET...

AND OUR PARENTS CAN'T AFFORD THE DRUGS SOLD IN THE PHARMACY?

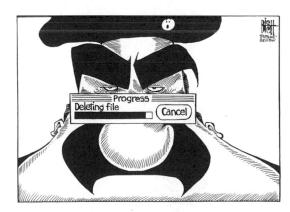

Randy Bish
622 Cabin Hill Drive
Greensburg, PA 15601
724-834-1151
rbish@tribweb.com

Attack of the Political Cartoonists 19

Tom Bone

Tom Bone is both the editorial cartoonist and a full-time sports writer for the *Bluefield Daily Telegraph* in his native state of West Virginia. Since 1996 he has also provided editorial cartoons for the weekly *Princeton Times*, a sister newspaper. He also creates occasional maps and graphics for the *Telegraph* and has covered federal court trials as a courtroom artist.

Bone's artwork has won four first-place awards in the West Virginia Press Association annual competition.

He is a graduate of Concord College and Marshall University. Prior to joining the *Telegraph*, he taught school for a year, worked at a Huntington, West Virginia, television station, and spent 20 years in college public relations.

Tom Bone
tbone@bdtonline.com

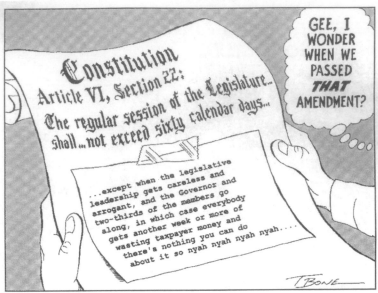

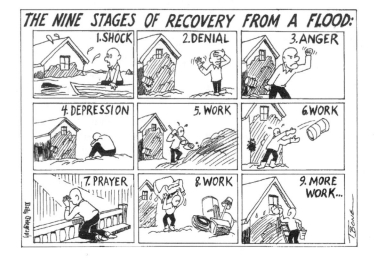

Insights & Assaults from Today's Editorial Pages

John Branch

John Branch began his career in his home town at the *Chapel Hill Newspaper* in 1976, the same year he graduated from the University of North Carolina with a degree in studio art.

He has been the editorial cartoonist for the *San Antonio Express-News* since 1981.

His work is syndicated by King Features in its "Best and Wittiest" package. Branch's cartoons have been reprinted in *The New York Times, USA Today, Newsweek* and numerous other publications.

A former officer of the Association of American Editorial Cartoonists, Branch has published two collections of his work, "Out on a Limb" and "Would You Buy a Used Cartoon from This Man?"

He and his wife Lynn Gosnell have two children, Adrien and James.

John Branch
jbranch@express-news.net
www.mysanantonio.com

Steve Breen

Born in 1970 in Los Angeles, Steve Breen grew up in neighboring Orange County as the second oldest of eight children. He graduated from Huntington Beach High School in 1988 and attended the University of California at Riverside, where he earned a bachelor's degree in political science.

It was at the university that he started drawing editorial cartoons for his school paper, *The Highlander*. In 1991, Breen won both the Scripps Howard Charles M. Schulz Award as the top college cartoonist and the John Locher award for Outstanding College Editorial Cartoonist.

Breen was about to become a high-school history teacher when New Jersey's *Asbury Park Press* offered him a job in the art department in July 1994. He became the full-time editorial cartoonist there in 1996, and in April 1998 won the Pulitzer Prize for editorial cartooning.

In July 2001, Breen returned to his home state to join the staff of *The San Diego Union-Tribune*. His editorial cartoons are nationally syndicated by Copley News Service and regularly appear in *The New York Times, USA Today, Newsweek* and *US News and World Report*. His comic strip "Grand Avenue" appears in more than 150 newspapers across the country.

Breen lives in the San Diego area with his wife Cathy and their two young sons. He enjoys reading, running, playing the guitar, and watching old movies on cable.

Steve Breen
steve.breen@uniontrib.com

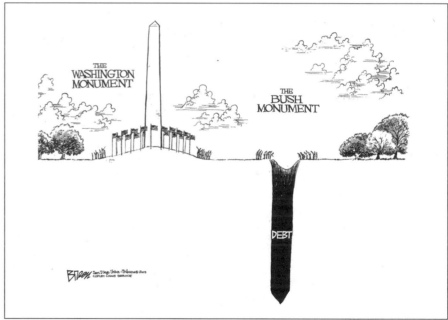

OVER A BARREL

Chris Britt

Chris Britt is the editorial cartoonist for the *State Journal Register* in Springfield, Illinois. His cartoons are syndicated by Copley News Service to newspapers around the country.

Britt has also worked for the *Arizona Business Gazette, the Sacramento Union, the Houston Post, the News Tribune* in Tacoma, Washington, and *the Seattle Times*.

His cartoons have been published in *Newsweek, Newsweek Japan, Time, US News and World Report, The New York Times, The Washington Post* and *USA Today.* They have been aired on CNN's "Inside Politics" and ABC's "Good Morning America."

In 1994, Britt was named Cartoonist of the Year by the National Press Foundation in Washington, D.C. He has also won press club awards in Texas, California, Washington State and Illinois.

Chris Britt was born in Phoenix, Arizona, in 1959, and now lives with his wife Nicky and their daughter Emily in Springfield. When he is not hacking off readers, he can be found hacking a golf ball around the links.

**Chris Britt
One Copley Plaza
Springfield, IL 62705**

Stan Burdick

Stan Burdick got his start a long, long time ago by winning several cartoon contests in an early boys' magazine titled *Open Road for Boys*. He later co-edited and co-published *American Square Dance* magazine, which helped hone his drawing and writing skills.

His interest in editorial cartooning began with several works published by the *Sandusky Register* in Ohio and other journals. Retirement to New York in the early 1990's offered Stan the opportunity to do serious editorial cartooning, and he provided work to the *Post Star* in Glenn Falls, and the *Press Republican* in Plattsburgh. He currently is the staff cartoonist of *Lake Champlain Weekly* in Plattsburgh.

Stan founded and directs the activities of A Cartoon Museum in Ticonderoga (formerly located in Hague, New York), where over 500 comic and editorial cartoons are exhibited for public viewing.

A member of both the AAEC and National Cartoonist Society, Stan resides with his wife Cathie at Silver Bay, New York, on Lake George. His honors for cartoon work include five one-man art shows in area galleries, the Adirondack Park "Outstanding Communicator" Award in 2000, and inclusion in "Best Editorial Cartoons of the Year" in 2003.

Stan Burdick
1 Burdick Lane
Silver Bay, NY 12874
518-543-8824

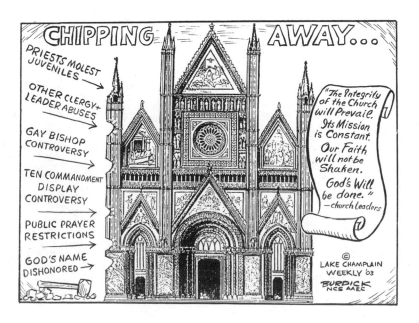

Daryl Cagle

Daryl Cagle is the editorial cartoonist for Slate.com, Microsoft's opinion magazine. His cartoons appear in over 600 newspapers, and his web site, "Daryl Cagle's Professional Cartoonists' Index" (www.cagle.slate.msn.com) is one of the most popular cartoon sites on the web. It currently features the work of 200 editorial cartoonists and is used in classrooms around the world.

Cagle attended college at the University of California at Santa Barbara before moving to New York City, where he worked for ten years with Jim Henson's Muppets, drawing pigs, frogs, Fraggles, and Sesame Street characters on all manner of products and books. After his Muppet years, Cagle worked as a toy inventor, licensing his concepts to scores of toy companies including "My Magic Genie" dolls for Hasbro and designs for Mattel, Playskool, Milton Bradley, Fisher-Price and others.

He has won "Best Advertising Cartoonist of the Year" from the National Cartoonists Society, and is a past president of the NCS.

Before partnering with Microsoft, Cagle was a daily editorial cartoonist for Gannett's *Honolulu Advertiser* newspaper. In the 1990s, he drew a syndicated panel cartoon called "TRUE" for Tribune Media Services.

Daryl lives with his wife Peg, daughter Susie and son Buster in Los Angeles.

Daryl Cagle
cari@cagle.com
slate.msn.com

Gordon Campbell

Born and raised in southern California, Gordon Campbell has been riding the crest of America's political storm waves since, like, forever, dude. His first cartoons appeared in various area college newspapers beginning in the late 60s, mainly because his attendance at area colleges was, well, various. Always an under-achieving student of history and politics, his illustrations described those turbulent days with a depth of knowledge and a sense of the absurd that few of his less politically minded friends appreciated. "Get into plastics," they said. "Draw for Disney." Choosing, instead, to heed the encouragement from many editors, publishers and other ink-stained wretches he encountered around the Golden State, Campbell continued to swim out beyond the breakwater of reason in search of the perfect graphic image.

Decades later, Campbell is still getting ink on his hands and the traditional shark-like hate letters (now in the e-mail version) that are the hallmarks of the working staff political cartoonist. In 1996, Campbell's cartoons brought his paper a first place award in the California Newspaper Publishers Association's annual "Better Newspapers" contest. His efforts appear most days in the *Inland Valley Daily Bulletin* in Ontario, California, and are available around the Southland to papers in the Los Angeles Newspaper Group, part of the vast Media News empire.

Gordon Campbell
2041 E. 4th St.
Ontario, CA 91764
909-483-9315
g_campbell@dailybulletin.com

THE TAX POOL PRIMORDIAL

FITTING THE PROFILE!

SOMETHING SURVIVES!

DRAGGING THE WORLD TO WAR!

Stu Carlson

As a youngster growing up in West Bend, Wisconsin, Stuart Carlson exhibited a knack for cartooning at a tender age, sometimes drawing on the walls of his parents' apartment with lipstick.

Before joining the *Milwaukee Journal Sentinel* in 1983, Carlson was a reporter, cartoonist and editor for a weekly newspaper and a small daily in Wisconsin. His work is currently syndicated to more than 50 newspapers nationwide by Universal Press Syndicate.

Carlson's ability to translate current events into cogent visual statements has won him several awards, including the 1995 John Fischetti award, numerous best-cartoon-of-the-year honors from the Milwaukee Press Club, and was named the nation's best cartoonist in 1991 by the National Press Foundation.

Carlson lives in a maintenance-intensive Victorian house in Milwaukee with his wife Mary, daughters Caitlin and Bridget, and son, Brendan.

Stu Carlson
scarlson@journalsentinel.com

James Casciari

James Casciari pens his award winning creations of comment for *the Vero Beach Press Journal* and its various sister properties: *the Stuart News, Naples Daily News, Ft. Pierce Tribune, Sebastian Sun* and *the Port St. Lucie News*. In addition, he contributes regularly to Florida's other major dailies and several national weekly roundups.

Casciari's work is distributed by the Scripps Howard News Service to almost 400 newspapers worldwide. National clients include *The Washington Post, the National Forum, Newsweek, USA Today, American City Business Journals*, and McGraw-Hill Publishing.

Casciari began his career drawing editorial cartoons at the University of Miami in Coral Gables, Florida, for the university newspaper *The Hurricane*.

His work has appeared in Pelican Publishing's "Best Editorial Cartoons of the Year," as well as Pineapple Press' "Florida's Best Editorial Cartoons."

He is a five-time recipient of the Florida Press Club's Excellence in Journalism Award for editorial cartooning, and was the winner of the 2001 Scripps Howard Foundation National Journalism Award.

When not drawing editorial cartoons or busy with freelance graphic design and illustration, he enjoys college football, fishing and fiddling with his antique sports car. He is married and resides on Vero Beach's Orchid Island.

James Casciari
P.O. Box 3701
Vero Beach, FL 32964
772-234-1951
JCasciari@aol.com

M.e. Cohen

M.e. Cohen's daily political cartoons appear regularly in the *Daily Record* of Morristown, New Jersey, as well as several other New Jersey newspapers.

He has been a professional illustrator since 1983 and has drawn over 5,000 illustrations for major publications worldwide.

Highlights of his career include the long-running publication of his business editorial cartoon "Bottom Dollar" in New York's *Newsday,* several national awards as an advertising art director, teaching his "Smart Art" approach to illustration at the School of Visual Arts in New York City, and working as an editorial Art Director.

The lights of his life, wife Claudia and two sons, Sebastien and August, fill all his time away from the drawing board.

**M.e. Cohen
28 Aubrey Rd.
Upper Montclair, N.J. 07043
973-783-1171
M.e.@humorink.com
www.humorink.com**

John Cole

Born in Rochester, New York, and raised in Lexington, Kentucky, John Cole graduated in 1980 with a degree in journalism from

Washington and Lee University in Lexington, Virginia. Advised by one of his professors that no one would pay him real U.S. currency for "drawing funny pictures," he started his newspaper career in Greenup, Kentucky, covering local government and county-fair baby-beauty contests. Later, he worked as a reporter, photographer, feature editor, illustrator and sometime cartoonist for a small afternoon daily in Danville, Kentucky.

He joined the staffs of the former *Durham Morning Herald* and *the Durham Sun* in 1985, and as graphics editor oversaw their appearance and design when they merged into *The Herald-Sun* in 1991. He has been drawing editorial cartoons on a five-times-a-week basis since 1992. In addition to various press association awards for writing, photography, illustration and design, he received an honorable mention in the 1994 Fischetti Editorial Cartoon Competition and won first place in the Fischetti in 2004. His first collection of cartoons, "Politics, barbecue & balderdash," was published in the fall of 1995.

Cole lives with his wife Kate and daughter Caroline in Durham, North Carolina.

John Cole
P.O. Box 2092
Durham, NC 27702
919-419-6741
www.heraldsun.com/opinion/

[Campaign tactics adapt to low turnout in local elections.]

Ed Colley

Ed Colley is the editorial cartoonist for the *Boston Globe South & Globe Northwest.* He has also drawn for the Memorial Press Group out of Plymouth, Massachussets, and freelanced for Beacon Community Newspapers.

Colley has been awarded First Place in Editorial Cartooning from Suburban Newspapers of America, and from 1990 to 2001, his work appeared regularly in "Best Editorial Cartoons of the Year."

From 1990 to 1999 Colley's strip "Suburban Cowgirls" was syndicated through Tribune Media Services to over 100 newspapers, and were collected together and published by Andrew and McMeel in two volumes: "Suburban Cowgirls" and "A Fist Full of Credit Cards."

Ed Colley
ecolley372@attbi.com

[A campaign against a smoking ban in Middleborough has a patriotic theme.]

F. James Corwin

F. James Corwin was born in Newton, Massachusetts, and moved to Martha's Vineyard Island at the age of three weeks, where she was raised by her namesakes, Frances and James MacInnis. After graduating from Tisbury High School, she attended the School of the Museum of Fine & Applied Arts in Boston. She also studied Portraiture with Joan Trimble-Smith at the Framingham Civic Art League, Regis College and privately at the Trimble-Smith Studio in Wayland, Massachusetts.

In 1971, Corwin started sketching portraits in public at the Boston Flea Market as a way to pay for her space. Over the years, she's sketched in many juried art shows, state fairs, church fairs, street fairs, art fairs, and malls, and has received numerous awards for her art work and photography, mainly in the Boston area.

In 1992, Corwin started drawing editorial cartoons for *The Valley Comic News* in the Northampton area, starting with panels titled "The Right Side," "The Washington Fat Cats" and "The Mother Lode of Motherland."

After moving to Florida in 1994, Corwin started drawing editorial cartoons for the Forum section of the Wednesday edition of the *Englewood Sun Herald.* Corwin's cartoons have also appeared several times on C-Span's "Washington Journal."

David Cox

After watching Gov. Bill Clinton's Democratic response to the Ronald Reagan's 1985 State of the Union address, Texan David Cox drew a cartoon on the subject and sent it to the local paper, the *Plano Daily Star Courier*. The editor called and asked Cox if he would submit cartoons on a weekly basis.

Over the next few years Cox sent his cartoons to newspapers throughout the country. He compiled an impressive stack of rejection letters, but he also eventually found one newspaper, *The Morning News* of Northwest Arkansas, that was willing to hire him as a reporter/cartoonist, and he went on to self-syndicate to about two dozen Arkansas newspapers for five years.

A year after taking a job as a reporter at the weekly *Cherokee Villager*, Cox was named managing editor; a year after that, he was the owner and publisher. During the next dozen years he garnered more than 150 state and national awards, mostly for editorials, humor columns, photography and investigative reporting.

He put away his brushes in 1995 to devote his full attention to publishing, but dug them out in 2000 when the *Arkansas Democrat-Gazette* called to offer him a full-time position as its number-two editorial cartoonist behind John Deering. He now draws five cartoons a week, working at night and on weekends, while he continues as managing editor of a group of weekly newspapers in Arkansas and Missouri.

He and his wife Heidi, a teacher and columnist, have five children.

David Cox
P.O. Box 480
Cherokee Village, AR 72525
870-257-2417
roundhouse@centurytel.net

J.D. Crowe

Soon after graduating from Eastern Kentucky University in 1981, J.D. Crowe was hired as a staff artist by the *Fort Worth Star-Telegram*. He was quickly shuffled into a vacated editorial cartoonist position after one of his cartoons for the news side brought threats of a libel suit. (It was a good editorial cartoon, *bad* news illustration, but it gave him his lucky break.)

After several award-winning years at the *Star-Telegram* and then the (now-defunct) *Tribune* in San Diego, California, Crowe launched a freelance career, drawing political cartoons primarily for the *Los Angeles Times* and *Sacramento Bee*. He also ventured into comic strips, travel writing and figure painting.

Crowe joined the *Mobile Register* in Alabama in 2000, where he now draws five editorial cartoons a week. His work is internationally syndicated by Artizans.com.

He has published two books of his work: "Daze of Glory: Images of Fact and Fantasy Inspired by the Gulf War" in 1991, and "Dark Side of the MoonPie" in 2003.

J.D. Crowe lives in Fairhope, Alabama, with his wife Lori, daughter Bronwen, two dogs and a cat and a half.

J.D. Crowe
P.O. Box 2488
Mobile, AL 36652
251-219-5676
jdcrowe@mobileregister.com

I HATE THAT IT'S EVERYWHERE...
T.V., MAGAZINES, NEWSPAPERS....

I HATE THAT OUR FREEDOMS
HAVE BEEN COMPROMISED.

I HATE THAT A YEAR LATER,
I STILL HAVE THE SAME ANXIETIES
I FELT ON THAT DAY.

I HATE THAT AIRPORT SECURITY
IS STILL A JOKE.

I HATE 9/11 MEMORIAL
MERCHANDISE.

MORE THAN 3,000 INNOCENT
PEOPLE DIED IN THE ATTACKS.

I HATE THAT THE MOST.

Stacy Curtis

Stacy Curtis is the full-time editorial cartoonist for *The Times* of Northwest Indiana in Munster, Indiana. Curtis has won several awards including the Best of Indiana, Society

of Professional Journalists award.

His editorial cartoons are distributed to newspapers, magazines and other publications world-wide by Artizans. His work has also appeared in several magazines and newspapers across the United States, on the MSNBC web site and in the annual "Best Editorial Cartoons of the Year" collections by Pelican Publishing.

Curtis sat in on the comic strip, "Non Sequitur" while the strip's creator, Wiley Miller, was on vacation in November 1998.

Stacy Curtis
601 45th Ave.
Munster, IN 46321
scurtis@nwitimes.com
www.stacycurtis.com

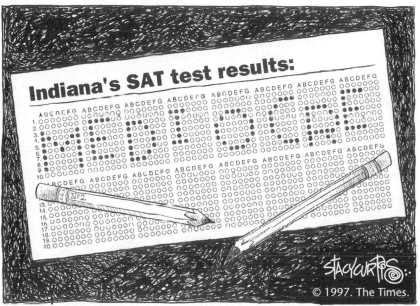

Charlie Daniel

Charlie Daniel (no "S" on Daniel, please) was born in Richmond, Virginia, and grew up (physically) in Weldon, North Carolina. After attending Fork Union Military Academy, he was a private in the Marine Corps and a major in political science at the University of North Carolina.

He started cartooning for *The Daily Tar Heel* at UNC when a friend convinced him that he didn't really want a lot of money and a career in business. He joined *The Knoxville Journal* as editorial cartoonist in 1958 and moved to *The Knoxville News Sentinel* on January 1, 1992.

Charlie Daniel and his childhood sweetheart, Patsy Stephenson, married and have two children, three grandchildren and too many cats.

Charlie Daniel
865-342-6253
daniel@knews.com

Matt Davies

Born in London in 1966, Matt Davies moved to the U.S. in 1983. After studying at the Savannah College of Art & Design in Georgia, and the School of Visual Arts in New York City, he began a freelance illustration career which quickly descended into days spent drawing bad editorial cartoons for some weekly newspapers that nobody's heard of, with the exception, perhaps, of *The Village Voice*.

Nevertheless, Davies somehow managed to get hired full-time to draw editorial cartoons in 1993 with Gannett's *The Journal News* in leafy Westchester County, New York. He is still there, though he is now also syndicated by Tribune Media Services.

His cartoons are reprinted occasionally.

In 2004, Davies won both the inaugural Herblock Prize and the Pulitzer Prize for Editorial Cartooning.

He also won the 2000 Robert F. Kennedy award, which his wife, Lucy, is very proud of.

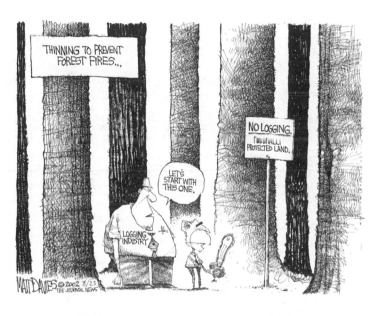

Matt Davies
914-696-8159
mdavies@thejournalnews.gannett.com

Justin DeFreitas

Justin DeFreitas is the editorial cartoonist for the *Berkeley Daily Planet* in California. His work is also self-syndicated to more than a dozen newspapers and magazines in Northern California.

He began his cartooning career at the University of California at Santa Cruz with a comic strip called "The Eighth Circle." The strip won a Columbia Gold Circle Award for Best Humorous Cartoon in 1997.

After graduating, he turned to political cartooning, winning the 2003 James Madison Freedom of Information Award for Editorial Cartooning for images dealing with the threat posed to the First Amendment by the Bush administration and the war on terrorism.

DeFreitas's cartoons have also appeared in the *Los Angeles Times*, the *Foreign Service Journal*, and "Best Editorial Cartoons of the Year."

Justin DeFreitas
3023A Shattuck Avenue
Berkeley, Ca. 94705
510-841-5600
defreitas@jfdefreitas.com
www.jfdefreitas.com

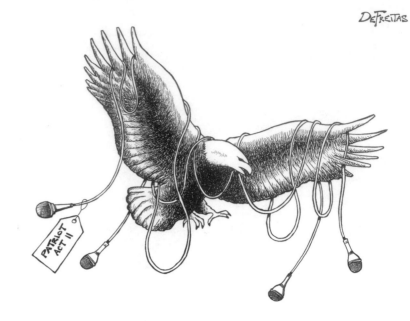

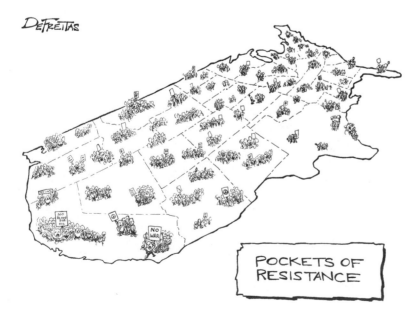

POCKETS OF RESISTANCE

IRAQ OCCUPATION: A WEEK AT A GLANCE

Bill DeOre

Bill DeOre joined *The Dallas Morning News* in 1970 as an advertising artist. In 1971, he became the art director of the newspaper's Sunday magazine, and has been its editorial cartoonist since January 1, 1977.

He draws five editorial cartoons each week for the *Morning News* and is nationally syndicated by Universal Press Syndicate. His cartoons have been featured in *the New York Times, the Washington Post, USA Today* and *Newsweek*. Many politicians — including Presidents George W. Bush, George Bush Sr., Gerald Ford and Jimmy Carter — have requested originals of his cartoons.

He has won nine Katie Awards from the Press Club of Dallas for outstanding editorial cartoons, and in 1983, DeOre received the Fischetti Award for best editorial cartoon.

He is the proud father of two sons, Will and Patrick, and is also active in the community, serving as a Jesuit Art Museum trustee and on the board of directors of the Jesuit Alumni Association.

Bill DeOre
5939 Elderwood Dr.
Dallas, TX 75230
214-977-8257
bdeore@dallasnews.com

Dennis Draughon

Dennis Draughon was born in 1961 and spent the first 29 years of his life in Virginia and North Carolina before moving to Pennsylvania to work for the *Scranton Times.*

In 1979, in a scene reminiscent of a driver's education film, Draughon's car stalled on the tracks in the path of an oncoming train. Coming to consciousness later with the locomotive occupying the passenger seat, Draughon patted the throbbing engine and said, "Nice train, don't finish me off now." Suffering only a minor cut, he went back to school the next day.

Draughon attended North Carolina State University after failing the physical exam for West Point as one of Sen. Jesse Helms' appointees. He studied history while serving for eight years as editorial cartoonist for the student newspaper, *The Technician.*

After a brief sojourn making rope hammocks at Twin Oaks commune in Virginia, Draughon was hired in 1985 as the last cartoonist for the now defunct *Raleigh Times.* Since 1990, he has drawn daily editorial cartoons for the *Scranton Times.*

His work has earned a Fischetti Award for Distinguished Achievement in 1993 and the Association of American Editorial Cartoonists' "Golden Spike" in 1999. In his spare time, Draughon reads copiously and enjoys spending time with his wife Megan and kids Frances and Charlie.

Dennis Draughon
ddraughon@timesshamrock.com

IF POLITICIANS HAD TO DISPLAY THEIR SPONSORS LIKE ATHLETES DO

Peter Dunlap-Shohl

Peter Dunlap-Shohl has worked as cartoonist for the *Anchorage Daily News* for over 20 years, producing four editorial cartoons per week, concentrating mostly on local topics.

For the past 12 years he has also written and drawn an Alaska-based comic strip, "Muskeg Heights," that appears six times a week in the *Daily News.* He has won awards from organizations including the Alaska Press Club, the Society of Newspaper Design and the Society of Professional Journalists, which awarded him first place in its 2002 Northwest regional editorial cartoon competition.

Dunlap-Shohl has lived most of his life in Anchorage, surviving the largest earthquake ever recorded in North America, the Exxon Valdez oil spill, sundry volcanic eruptions and moose charges. He lives in the foothills of the Chugach Mountains with his wife Pamela and son Wiley. His hobbies include mountain biking, skiing and playing the dobro.

Peter Dunlap-Shohl
907-257-4364
dunlap-shohl@gci.net

$97.03, PLUS TAX.

I'M SURE GLAD WE'RE NOT PUNISHING HARD-WORKING, PRODUCTIVE SUCCESSES WITH AN INCOME TAX.

ALASKA SOLUTIONS TO THE BALLISTIC MISSILE THREAT

DOMED CITIES: WE COULD GET THE PLANS FROM MIKE GRAVEL!

ROCKET-EQUIPPED BUSH PILOTS: WE COULD GET THE MONEY FROM TED STEVENS!

SYNCHRONIZED HANDGUN FIRE: IT WOULDN'T WORK, BUT NEITHER DOES MISSILE DEFENSE.

[Peter Dunlap-Shohl explains the local cartoon to the left: "OK, this one is arcane, but it covers a bunch of ground, sending up the ludicrousity of the missile defense system, our dependence on Federal money, and our passion for guns. Mike Gravel was a U.S. Senator from Alaska who proposed building a domed city for our Capital, and Ted Stevens is our senior Senator, who, as chairman of the Senate Appropriations Committee, has steered billions of dollars home. Hope this helps."]

Bob Englehart

Bob Englehart has been the editorial cartoonist for the nation's oldest newspaper, *The Hartford Courant,* since 1980. He has received awards from the Overseas Press Club, Planned Parenthood and the Free Press Association, and was a finalist for the Pulitzer Prize in 1979.

Englehart's cartoons have appeared in *USA Today, Time, Newsweek, the New York Times, the Washington Post, the London Times* and *Playboy.* He has authored two collections of his work and has been exhibited by the Connecticut Historical Society, Trinity College, The Old State House in Hartford and The Newseum in Washington D.C.

He and his wife Pat McGrath have worked together creating a comic strip called "Moo" and a weekly "video comic strip" about sports called "Last Row with Englehart and McGrath," which ran on ESPN every Sunday morning for five years. Englehart has also appeared in a Broadway political comedy review called "Raucous Caucus."

Englehart and McGrath live in Middletown, Connecticut, and together have three grown children and two grandchildren.

Bob Englehart
benglehart@courant.com
860-343-5222

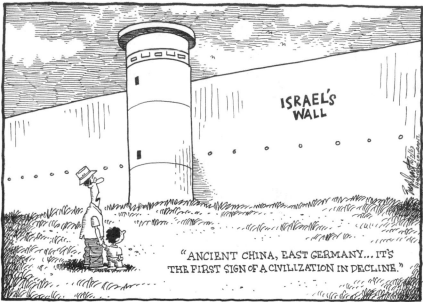

Brian Fairrington

A 1999 graduate of Arizona State University, Brian Fairrington earned a bachelors degree in political science and a masters degree in communications.

Fairrington is the recipient of the 1996 John Locher Memorial Award. He also received the Charles M. Schulz Award from the Scripps Howard Foundation as best college cartoonist of the year. Additionally, he is a two-time winner of the Mark of Excellence Award from the Society of Professional Journalists and a seven-time recipient of the Gold Circle Award from the Columbia Press Association. He also shared an Emmy award for his regular appearance on the Phoenix-based television show "Horizon."

Fairrington is currently a contributing cartoonist with the *Arizona Republic.* His cartoons are nationally syndicated to over 600 newspapers throughout America with Caglecartoons.com, and his work has appeared in *The New York Times* and *USA Today*.

Fairrington has also created illustrations for five books and numerous web sites.

He is married to Stacey Heywood Fairrington, a broadcast journalist. They have two children, Chase Alan, 3, and one-year-old Hayden Lyn.

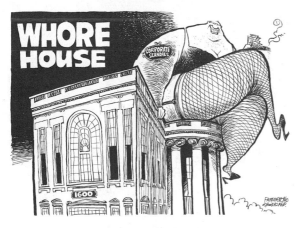

Brian Fairrington
480-720-2788
bfair97@aol.com
AtomicComicCafe.com

Paul Fell

Paul Fell grew up in Massachusetts and headed west to Nebraska to play football and go to college. Vowing never to return following graduation, he instead married a farm girl and is still there, over three decades later. (Now he thinks all those Easterners are crazy ... and they talk funny, too.)

Fell has been a high school art teacher and coach, and a college art professor. During his high school teaching days he started drawing editorial cartoons for small weekly newspapers in Nebraska, and in 1984 he joined the staff of the *Lincoln Journal* as editorial cartoonist and newsroom artist. That lasted until 1992 when a number of *Journal* employees were eliminated in an alleged cost-cutting move. Fell's position was the first to go.

Since then he has freelanced full time, creating three editorial cartoons each week for the *Lincoln Journal Star.* He also draws a cartoon for the Nebraska Press Association that is distributed to newspapers statewide. In addition, he draws sports cartoons for *Huskers Illustrated* magazine and humorous illustrations for a wide variety of clients in the Midwest and nationwide. He keeps his teaching skills sharpened by serving as a visiting lecturer in art from time to time at several of Nebraska's colleges and universities.

Fell's editorial cartoons have garnered a number of awards over the years. He has received recognition for his work from the National Newspaper Association, the Population Institute, the National Cartoonists Society, and the University of Nebraska, to name a few.

Fell continues to live in Lincoln, where he enjoys the slower pace and relative sanity of the Great Plains. His long-suffering wife, Arlene, continues her fruitless efforts to domesticate him.

Paul Fell
paulfellcartoons@alltel.net
www.paulfellcartoons.com

Row 1 (strip):
- YOUR BIRTHPLACE IS THE LUCK OF THE DRAW.
- I COULD HAVE BEEN BORN IN A RICH NATION WHERE I MIGHT HAVE ENDED UP AS THE WILDLY-WEALTHY C.E.O. OF A MULTINATIONAL CORPORATION.
- INSTEAD, I'M HERE IN A POOR COUNTRY WHERE ONE DAY MY FAMILY FARM WILL FAIL IN THE FACE OF GLOBALIZED TRADE, SO I'LL WORK IN A SWEATSHOP IF I CAN EVEN FIND A JOB.
- WANNA SELL DRUGS INSTEAD?
- THAT OR ARMED REVOLT.

Row 2 (strip):
- ONCE UPON A TIME IN AMERICA, BEFORE THE "IMPERIAL PRESIDENCY"...
- WE HAD A REAL CONGRESS.
- IT EVEN TOOK PART IN FOREIGN POLICY.
- YOU MEAN AMERICA USED TO BE A REPRESENTATIVE DEMOCRACY?

Row 3 (strip):
- BADGES?
- WE AIN'T GOT NO BADGES.
- WE DON'T NEED NO BADGES.
- I DON'T HAVE TO SHOW YOU ANY STINKING BADGES!

Row 4 (strip):
- BROTHERS AND SISTERS, I OPPOSE THE MARRIAGE OF IDEAS.
- AND I OPPOSE THE MARRIAGE OF WORDS AND MUSIC....AND THE MARRIAGE OF TRADITION AND INNOVATION...
- AND THE MARRIAGE OF MUSIC AND DANCE... AND THE MARRIAGE OF PAINTING AND POETRY... AND THE MARRIAGE OF COMPANIES.
- BECAUSE, BROTHERS AND SISTERS, MARRIAGE IS BETWEEN A MAN AND A WOMAN.

Row 5 (strip):
- I, GEORGE W. BUSH, AM THE ENVIRONMENTAL PRESIDENT.
- THAT'S A WRAP.

Charles Fincher

Charles Fincher moves back and forth between his career in cartooning and his career in law. In law, he is of counsel to The Allison Law Firm, a litigation boutique in Brownsville, Texas. Fincher also paints in oils and acrylics and occasionally writes for newspapers.

His political strip, "Thadeus & Weez," runs weekly on the opinion pages of the *Houston Chronicle, Austin American-Statesman, Corpus Christi Caller-Times, Fort Worth Star-Telegram* (comics page), *Valley Morning Star, Odessa American, Sherman Democrat* and *Tyler Morning Telegraph.* Online, the strip appears in the *Houston Chronicle, Corpus Christi Caller-Times, Flak Magazine, Jewish World Review, Odessa American* and *Amarillo Globe-News.*

Fincher lives and works three miles off the Texas coast on South Padre Island. On the island, he jogs and works out with his girlfriend, trial lawyer Dana Allison, who is also the head of his law firm.

They also do low-energy island stuff as well, like just enjoying life on a beach.

Charles Fincher
charles.fincher@thadeusandweez.com

Mark Fiore

Mark Fiore's animated political cartoons appear on news web sites across the country and are seen by millions, possibly even scrillions. Formerly a print political cartoonist who did a stint at the *San Jose Mercury News*, Fiore now focuses exclusively on animated political cartoons.

Fiore's commentaries *[frames of which are shown here]* appear regularly on the *San Francisco Chronicle's* SFGate.com, Salon.com, VillageVoice.com, Mother-Jones.com and many other news sites.

The Online News Association and the Columbia Graduate School of Journalism presented Fiore with the 2002 Online Journalism Award for commentary and nominated him for the same award in 2003. Fiore also received the National Cartoonists Society's New Media award for his work in animated political cartoons two years in a row.

Mark Fiore is also very uncomfortable referring to himself in the third person.

[Mark Fiore is the first political cartoonist we know of to leave print media completely behind. Whether this is a harbinger of things to come in the 21st Century or not remains to be seen. What is certain is his work — complete with music and sound effects — must be seen online to be fully appreciated, and we encourage readers to log on and check out one of the links below.]

USGS STUDY(rejiggered):
Caribou must do their part
in the Battle Against Evil.

Mark Fiore
550 Bryant Street
San Francisco, CA 94107
415-215-9557
www.markfiore.com
www.sfgate.com/comics/fiore

Jake Fuller

Jake Fuller was born in Lakeland, Florida, and went to the University of Florida, where he earned a B.S. in journalism, a B.A. in art and an MFA in fine arts. Since 1992, he has been employed by the *Gainesville Sun* as editorial cartoonist.

His work has won first place in the Sunshine State Awards in 2001 and 2002, first place from the Florida Press Club in 2001, third place in the 2001 Society of Professional Journalists Green Eyeshade Award, and an honorable mention in 2001 from The United Nation's Ranan Lurie Award.

He and his wife Laura have two sons.

Jake Fuller
fullerj@gvillesun.com

THE GHOST of DEFICITS PAST

Ed Gamble

Ed Gamble, a third generation journalist from a family of journalists, is in his 23rd year as editorial cartoonist for the *Florida Times-Union* and is starting his 29th year in national syndication with King Features Syndicate. His cartoons have been published in hundreds of newspapers and magazines around the world, including *The New York Times, the Washington Post, Los Angeles Times, Newsday, Dallas Morning News,* the *Chicago Tribune, the Denver Post,* and overseas in *LeMonde, the Independent,* and *Der Spiegel,* among others.

Gamble's cartoons have been exhibited overseas in China and at the American Center in Karachi, Pakistan. His cartoons are permanently displayed at the Texas Depository in Dallas, Texas, and at the Ford, Carter, Nixon, Reagan and Bush Presidential Museums.

A collection of Gamble's cartoons was published in 1996 by Pelican Publishing Company entitled "You Get Two For The Price Of One!" with the forewords written by former presidents Gerald Ford and George Bush. He also co-authored a book in 1988 with six other nationally recognized cartoonists.

Gamble earned a B.A. degree in political science at the University of South Florida. He and his wife, Saundra, have been married for 39 years and live in Mandarin, Florida.

Ed Gamble
egamble@jacksonville.com

"WHERE in this museum can I go to get away from your children?"

Anne Ganz

A geologist's daughter, Anne Ganz was born on the banks of the river Tigris in Iraq. She enjoyed a delightful nomadic childhood that left large holes in her education. No one told her that the Moulin Rouge is a darn windmill or that the Bridge of Sighs has nothing to do with matters of the heart, but leads from courtroom to dungeon. In 1966 she won the Kosciusko Foundation's Polish Millennium award for her large cartoon watercolor of Casimir the Great.

Her cartoons have appeared in *The Martha's Vineyard Comic Book, Madcap, Thorn* and *The Times of the Americas,* all of which have ceased to exist. She also drew a large cartoon map of Washington D.C. and caricatures of most of the media greats for the American News Women's Club.

Currently Ganz draws for *The Vineyard Gazette* and *The Vineyard Playhouse* on Martha's Vineyard, and is doing illustrations for a biography of the late White House reporter Sarah McClendon.

She is married and has four children and two grandchildren.

"I'm really looking forward to American bread with all those whipped in air bubbles."

Anne Ganz
3312 Lowell St., NW
Washington, D.C. 20008
202-966-9095
anne_ganz@yahoo.com

"Now, about the bundling, add to any amendment what's germane, and oh, how we s-t-r-e-t-c-h 'germane.'"

Bob Gorrell

Born and raised in Greensboro, North Carolina, Bob Gorrell attended the University of Virginia and graduated Phi Beta Kappa in 1977. After stints at the *Ft. Myers News-Press* in Florida, and the *Charlotte News* in North Carolina, he arrived at the *Richmond News Leader* in Virginia in 1983. Gorrell moved to the *Richmond Times-Dispatch* in 1992, and served there as editorial cartoonist until resigning in January 1998 to concentrate on syndicated editorial and comics-page features. In 2002, Gorrell was named the first-ever editorial cartoonist for America Online.

Gorrell's work has appeared through syndication in hundreds of newspapers, including *USA Today, the Washington Times, the Wall Street Journal* and *the New York Times.* His commentary has been featured in *Time, Newsweek, National Review* and other periodicals, and he has been a guest on CNN's "Crossfire" as well as other television and radio broadcasts.

His work has been cited for excellence by the Fischetti Editorial Cartoon Competition, the Overseas Press Club of America, and the Mencken Awards. In 1997, Gorrell received the National Press Foundation's Berryman Award as Editorial Cartoonist of the Year. His work has been included in numerous cartoon anthologies, and a collection of his cartoons titled "Affairs of State" was released in 1995.

Gorrell is married to Sabet Stroman and lives in Richmond, Virginia, where he and his wife work at raising their combined assortment of seven children.

Bob Gorrell
304 Long Lane
Richmond, Va 23221
804-254-2882
GorrellArt@aol.com

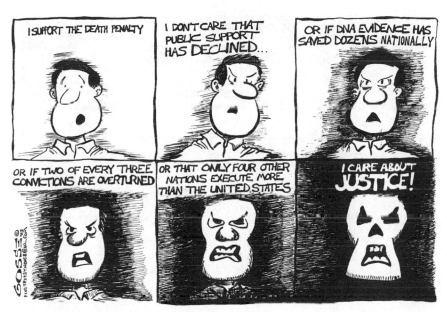

Ross Gosse

Born on the frozen tundra of Wisconsin, Ross Gosse earned his B.A. from the University of Wisconsin-Whitewater, where he double-majored in art and print journalism. His first job, in advertising, was disenchanting and disemboweling.

Heeding the noble call of journalism, Gosse landed his first daily newspaper job with *The Daily Press* in Ashland, Wisconsin, where he designed news pages and syndicated his editorial cartoons. Gosse then made a stop in Oil City, Pennsylvania, as a designer/graphic artist/illustrator with *The Derrick/The News-Herald* before heading to Ball State University in Muncie, Indiana. There, he drew cartoons for *The Daily News* school newspaper and earned his M.A. in journalism in May of 1999.

He interned that summer at *The Denver Post* where he designed graphics, drew sports cartoons and fulfilled a lifelong dream of being a mountain man.

By that fall, *The Plain Dealer* in Cleveland, Ohio, hired Gosse as a graphic artist. He won "Best in Ohio" for graphics and drank beer at Drew Carey's hangout, The Warsaw Tavern.

Gosse now lives in Locust, North Carolina, with his wife Susan, daughter Emma and dog Shea. When not washing bottles or changing diapers he syndicates his editorial cartoons statewide.

Ross Gosse
103 Old Hickory Rd.
Locust, NC 28097
PineTreeSyndic8@aol.com

Steve Greenberg

Steve Greenberg is an editorial cartoonist and graphic artist with the *Ventura County Star,* just northwest of Los Angeles in Southern California. He previously has worked for the *Daily News* of Los Angeles, *Seattle Post-Intelligencer, San Francisco Examiner, the San Francisco Chronicle* and *Marin Independent Journal,* and was the contributing editorial cartoonist for *Editor & Publisher* magazine from 1995 to 1998.

Greenberg's cartoons have won awards nearly every year of his career, including the 1994 Global Media Award for overpopulation cartoons (presented in Cairo, Egypt), the 1999 Homer Davenport contest Grand Prize, honors in the Free Press Association Mencken Awards, Washington Press Association and numerous regional Society of Professional Journalists competitions. He has also won Society of Newspaper Design awards for his graphics work.

His cartoons have been reprinted in *The New York Times, the Washington Post Weekly, Los Angeles Times,* and featured in numerous cartooning publications and books. His originals have been exhibited in cities and museums across the U.S. and Canada.

Greenberg is also a columnist for *Hogan's Alley* magazine. He has written for Disney comic books, has been a cartoonist/writer contributor to *Mad* magazine, and has a self-syndication service to Jewish newspapers nationwide.

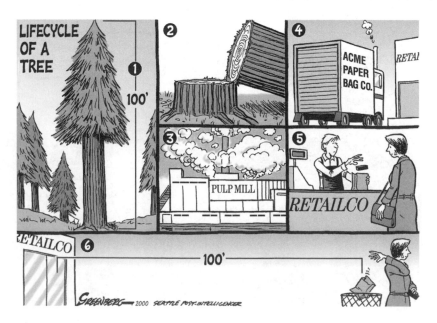

Steve Greenberg
steve@greenberg-art.com
www.greenberg-art.com

Ed Hall

Ed Hall has spent the last 15 years building a reputation as an editorial cartoonist with bite. He graduated from The University of Florida in 1986 with a Masters degree in Fine Art. While in college he did political cartoons and illustrations for UF's school paper *The Florida Independent Alligator.* After college, Hall worked for several weekly publications in and around Jacksonville, and finally settled at *The Baker County Press* in MacClenny, where he continues to work as the weekly cartoonist.

Over the last 11 years, Hall has won seven Florida Press Awards, three Newsmaker Awards and numerous fine art awards in national and international competitions. In 2003, he was presented the 53rd Annual Green Eyeshade Award for weekly cartoons by The Society of Professional Journalists, and the Excellence in Journalism Award from The Florida Press Club.

Through his weekly syndication with DBR Media, Hall's work is reproduced in newspapers across North America. In 2003 Hall joined Artizans Syndicate.

His cartoons have been featured in *The Washington Post National Weekly Edition, the Tallahassee Democrat,* and *the New York Time's Scope Magazine.* His work regularly appears in "Best Editorial Cartoons of the Year," and was part of the 2003 anthology on Bill Clinton titled "Hail to the Thief."

Ed Hall
www.Halltoons.com
halltoons@aol.com

Walt Handelsman

Since February of 2001, Walt Handelsman has been the nationally syndicated editorial cartoonist for *Newsday*.

Before that, Handelsman worked for *The Times-Picayune* in New Orleans from 1989 to 2001, the *Scranton Times* in Pennsylvania from 1985 to 1989 and a chain of 13 award-winning Baltimore and Washington Suburban weeklies from 1982 to 1985.

Handelsman, 47, a graduate of The University of Cincinnati, creates cartoons that appear in over 300 newspapers around the country and internationally. He is the winner of many local and national awards for cartooning excellence, including the 1989 and 1993 National Headliner Award, the 1992 Society of Professional Journalists Sigma Delta Chi Award, The 1996 Robert F. Kennedy Journalism Award and the 1997 Pulitzer Prize.

He is the author of five collections of his editorial cartoons as well as a children's book published in 1995.

Handelsman's cartoons are frequently reprinted in *USA Today, the New York Times, the Washington Post, the Chicago Tribune* and *Newsweek*.

He lives with his wife and two sons in Woodbury, New York.

Walt.Handelsman
walt.handelsman@newsday.com

Phil Hands

Since the spring of 1998 Phil Hands has provided the *Grosse Pointe News,* a weekly newspaper serving six Metro Detroit suburbs, with thought-provoking cartoons for its editorial page.

He also spent four years drawing cartoons for the student newspaper of Kenyon College, the *Kenyon Collegian.* In May of 2003, Hands graduated cum laude from Kenyon with a bachelors degree in both political science and studio art. His study of politics has given him a strong theoretical background with which to analyze politics, and his studies in studio art encouraged him to consider the most appealing way in which to display the political scenarios that he thinks he understands.

Despite being "big-boned," Hands is an avid skier. He is also a pathetically loyal Detroit Tigers fan and still gets upset when they lose (read: glutton for emotional punishment). He lives in St. Clair Shores, Michigan, with his very understanding girlfriend Tricia and a #%*&ing cat named Sparky, while he desperately tries to find somebody who would be willing to pay him something resembling a living wage for his cartoons.

Phil Hands
1150 Griswold, Suite 2800
Detroit MI, 48226
phil@philtoons.com
www.philtoons.com

[Mayor Kwame Kilpatrick of Detroit, above, came under fire when several members of his excessive security staff resigned because of allegations of corruption.]

Donna Hardy

Donna Hardy is a freelance cartoonist and humor illustrator. Her pen name, "Donnaree," is a childhood nickname that her family and friends use to this day. Hardy lives with her husband and three children on a farm in eastern North Carolina, along with their dog, two cats, five horses, bantam chickens and pet cockatiel.

In 1995, Hardy started drawing editorial cartoons for small area newspapers. She eventually joined the staff of one of her clients, the *Kinston Free Press*, and worked as a news photographer and editorial cartoonist until 2001.

Carolina Country, a rural electric cooperative magazine, published the first of Hardy's many trade cartoons and illustrations in 1998. Its parent organization, the National Rural Electric Cooperative Association continues to distribute her work nationally as part of its industry media kit.

Hardy's editorial cartoons and illustrations have appeared in many other Freedom newspapers, the *Carolina Journal* and the Glencoe/McGraw-Hill textbook, "Local Government in North Carolina."

Donna Hardy
www.donnaree.com

"Now let's see what this baby can do."

["The Global TransPark in eastern North Carolina seeks to replicate the earlier success of the Research Triangle Park," Hardy says about the above local cartoon. "Like its predecessor, the TransPark has not produced overnight success, which has caused faltering financial support at the state level."]

Vic Harville

Vic Harville, a veteran political and sports cartoonist, joined Stephens Media Group in June 2000 after 12 years with the *Arkansas Democrat-Gazette*. His work has won several awards and honors.

Three books of his cartoons have been published. The first, "That's The Way To Run A War," was a collection of cartoons recounting the Persian Gulf War. The original artwork from the books cover now hangs in the George Bush Presidential Library on the campus of Texas A&M in College Station.

His second book, "We Knew Bill Clinton," was published in 1993, and featured a collection of Harville's work related to Clinton's 1992 presidential campaign. A third book, "Rounding Up the Usual Suspects," was released in early 2002.

Harville and his wife Jean live in North Little Rock, Arkansas.

Vic Harville
401 S. Victory
Little Rock, AR 72201
501-374-0699
vharville@arkansasnews.com

R.C. Harvey

R.C. Harvey is a freelance cartoonist and comics historian. He has cartooned in all the medium's forms — comic strips, gag cartoons, and comic books, as well as editorial cartoons.

At present, he operates a mail-order caricature service from his studio in Champaign, Illinois. He also researches the history of cartooning and has written several books on aspects of the subject. Harvey has contributed numerous cartoonists' biographies to Oxford University Press's "American National Biography" (both online and in print) and has written over 150 short biographies of cartoonists for "A Gallery of Rogues: Cartoonists' Self-caricatures," published by the Ohio Statue University Cartoon Research Library in 1998.

He also runs a website at www.RCHarvey.com, where he reviews graphic novels, reprint collections and books, and posts news and lore about cartooning.

Harvey often signs his work by affixing a tiny spectacled rabbit. He calls the rabbit Cahoots, but that's not his name. (His name, as anyone knows who remembers a Jimmy Stewart movie about a six-foot pooka, is Harvey. R.C. is only five-foot-eleven but he has aspirations.)

R.C. Harvey
2701 Maplewood Drive
Champaign, IL 61821
217-356-1406
RCHarvey@worldnet.att.net
www.RCHarvey.com

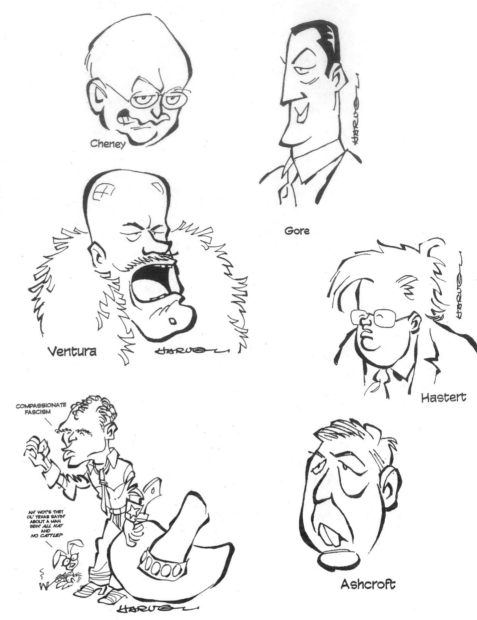

Joe Heller

Joe Heller is the editorial cartoonist for the *Green Bay Press-Gazette*, a position he's held since 1985. Before the *Press-Gazette*, he was cartoonist for the *West Bend News* in Wisconsin for five years. Heller's work is self-syndicated to more than 250 newspapers throughout the nation and regularly appears in the *Wisconsin State Journal, the Chicago Tribune, the Denver Post, the Washington Post, the Spokane Spokesman-Review* and *the Boston Globe*. His cartoons have also been reprinted in *Newsweek, Time, National Review, the Christian Science Monitor, the New York Times* and *the New Republic*.

He has won eight Best of Gannett awards for editorial cartoons, five Milwaukee Press Club awards and three Honorable mentions in the John Fischetti Editorial Cartoons Awards.

Heller has one book of his cartoons titled "Give 'Em Heller," published in 1991.

Born in Oshkosh, Wisconsin and raised in Milwaukee, Joe Heller is a graduate of the University of Wisconsin-Milwaukee with a B.A. in fine arts. He currently resides in Green Bay with his wife Pamela and their two daughters.

Joe Heller
joe@hellertoon.com

Draper Hill

Draper Hill is both a political cartoonist and a leading cartoon scholar, with a special interest in Thomas Nast. A native of Boston, he graduated from Harvard in 1957 and was hired by the *Patriot Ledger* in Quincy, Massachusetts. He later worked for the *Worchester Telegram, Memphis Commercial Appeal,* and, from 1976 to 1999, *the Detroit News.*

He now lives in Grosse Pointe, Michigan, with his wife Sarah and contributes editorial cartoons to the *Oakland Press* in Pontiac, Michigan.

Hill served as president of the Association of American Editorial Cartoonists in 1975-1976, and was awarded the Thomas Nast Prize by the city of Landau, Germany, in 1990.

His books include a biography of English cartoonist James Gillray, two collections of Gillray's etchings, and a collection of his own cartoons, "Political Asylum." He is currently completing a book on Nast and the Tweed Ring.

Draper Hill
368 Washington Rd.
Grosse Pointe, MI 48230
313-885-5435

.Hodin ©'02
apologies to Michelangelo

Russell W. Hodin

Russell Hodin was born in 1954 in Santa Monica, California, to William Joseph, Systems Engineer, and Margit Elisabeth, graduate of the Chicago Art Institute.
He studied engineering, fine arts and architecture before taking time out to travel across the U.S. and Europe to Nepal. He has worked as a carpenter, architect, illustrator, graphic artist, exhibition designer, and sculptor.
Since 1992, Hodin has been a weekly contributor to the local independent *New Times* in San Luis Obispo, California. His work was recognized by the National Newspaper Association in 1998, and the California Newspaper Publishers Association in 1996 and 1997.
He is married to Elizabeth Johnson.

Russell Hodin
hodin_ink@hotmail.com

Man, I sure hope you're puttin' in CRUELTY-FREE Regular 'Cuz my KARMA can't handle any of that ANGRY gas!

DIESEL PREMIUM REGULAR

GOD BLESS AMERICA

Joe Hoffecker

Joe Hoffecker was born in 1964 in Cincinnati, Ohio, and began drawing at a very early age. When shown an editorial cartoon at age 12, he knew then what his life's passion would be. While in high school, Hoffecker's art teacher introduced him to his best friend, Jim Borgman, the Pulitzer Prize-winner cartoonist for the *Cincinnati Enquirer.* Under Borgman's encouragement, Hoffecker began submitting drawings to his high school newspaper, which helped lead to an art scholarship to Northern Kentucky University.

In 1987, Hoffecker landed a job in the art department at the *Cincinnati Business Courier* and has been its editorial cartoonist ever since. Hoffecker's work has appeared in several sister publications of the *Business Courier*, including the *Sports Business Journal,* a national publication from Street & Smith. His work has also been published in the *Cincinnati Post* and *Enquirer.*

Hoffecker has won numerous awards for his cartoons, including prizes from the Cleveland Press Club and Society of Professional Journalists.

When not cartooning, Hoffecker enjoys spending time with his wife Tracy and daughters Katie, Maggie and Annie.

Joe Hoffecker
101 W. Seventh St.
Cincinnati, OH 45202
513-621-6665
jhoffecker@bizjournals.com

IRAQ OR BUST !

Jim Hope

Jim Hope is the editorial cartoonist for *The Culpeper News,* a weekly newspaper in Virginia with a circulation of 10,000.

From an early age, Hope was fascinated by art. His grandmother was a painter who traveled the world, grasping the artistic cultural from each place she visited. Her artistic influence on Hope began when she took him to art shows and introduced him to the different medias and styles, thus paving the way for his vivid imagination.

In high school, Hope drew cartoons for the school newspaper, and he later landed a job as a pressman with *The Culpeper Star Exponent* in Virginia. As time went on the newspaper gave him the opportunity to fulfill his dream and begin drawing editorial cartoons.

He still continues to paint and draw, and has entered his work in numerous art shows that have earned him first, second and third place finishes.

Jim Hope resides in historic Fredericksburg, Virginia, with his lovely wife Shirley, daughter Amy, son Jim, Jr., and three grandchildren.

Jim Hope
3 Kelly Ct
Fredericksburg, VA 22407
cameraman5@aol.com

David Horsey

David Horsey is the long-running editorial cartoonist for the *Seattle Post-Intelligencer*. His work is syndicated by Tribune Media Services to 250 newspapers, including *The Washington Post, the New York Times, the Chicago Tribune* and *Los Angeles Times*.

Among his other honors, Horsey has received the National Press Foundation's 1998 Berryman Award for Cartoonist of the Year. He was a Pulitzer finalist in 1987, and has twice been awarded the Pulitzer Prize for Editorial Cartooning, in 1999 and 2003.

David Horsey received a bachelor's degree in communications from the University of Washington, where he was editor of the student newspaper, *The Daily*. He earned a master's degree in international relations from the University of Kent at Canterbury in England.

The cartoonist originally started out as a political reporter and columnist. Since then, the Society of Professional Journalists has given him a total of 13 first-place regional awards for cartooning, governmental reporting and spot news reporting, as well as the 1999 Susan Hutchison Bosch Award for outstanding achievement in journalism.

Horsey's career at the *Post-Intelligencer* has taken him to national political party conventions, presidential primaries, international economic and diplomatic conferences, the Olympics, Japan and Europe.

In 2000-2001, he served as president of the Association of American Editorial Cartoonists.

Horsey has published five collections of his professional work, including "One Man Show" in 1999, and 2003's "From Hanging Chad to Baghdad." In 1992 he co-edited an anthology, "Cartooning AIDS Around the World."

A fourth generation Washingtonian, David Horsey lives in the heart of Seattle with his wife Nole Ann, and his daughter and son, Darielle and Daniel.

David Horsey
DavidHorsey@seattlepi.com

Etta Hulme

Etta Hulme began training for her future calling as an editorial cartoonist in her childhood, studying politics, economics and human nature from behind the counter of the family grocery store in Somerville, Texas.

Hulme earned a degree in fine arts from the University of Texas at Austin and then boarded the train for California, where she worked in the animation department at Disney for two years. After that, she worked in commercial art in Dallas and Midland, taught at an art school in San Antonio, and drew "Red Rabbit" comic books in Chicago.

Her first venture into editorial cartooning came in the 1950s, after her marriage to Vernon Hulme and the birth of her first child, when she drew editorial cartoons for *The Texas Observer* in Austin.

Hulme began drawing for *The Fort Worth Star-Telegram* in 1972 and has been there ever since. Her cartoons are syndicated nationwide by Newspaper Enterprise Association.

The National Cartoonists Society named Hulme Best Editorial Cartoonist in 1982 and 1998. She is also a past president of the Association of American Editorial Cartoonists.

Hulme has four children, none of whom has been convicted of a felony, and five unusually beautiful and talented grandchildren.

Etta Hulme
4054 Shady Valley Dr.
Arlington, TX 76013
ehulme3@comcast.net

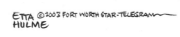

Tim Jackson

Tim Jackson, cartoonist, illustrator and graphic designer, is a Native of Dayton, Ohio. His childhood desire to be a cartoonist was first realized at the age of 14, when one of his cartoons appeared in the *Dayton Journal Herald.*

After a series of comic strips were printed in the *Dayton Daily News,* he was offered a weekend job with the *Dayton Black Press,* where he got hands-on experience in the actual production of the community newspaper.

Relocating to Chicago to attend the Art Institute of Chicago, Jackson majored in film, animation and art education.

In 1985 Jackson founded Creative License Studio, Inc., his own business to provide art services, and by 1990 he was syndicating cartoons to newspapers around the country, as well as publishing social awareness comic books that were distributed through Chicago Public Schools and the Chicago Department of Health.

Tim Jackson
www.CLStoons.com

Clay Jones

Clayton Jones currently works for *The Free Lance-Star* in Fredericksburg, Virginia, after doing a stint at the *Honolulu Star-Bulletin.* He started his career with *The Panolian,* a weekly newspaper in Batesville, Mississippi.

Jones has won state awards in Mississippi, Hawaii and Virginia.

While in Mississippi he self-syndicated his cartoons to over 40 newspapers; his work now is nationally distributed by Creators Syndicate.

His cartoons are archived at the Hattie Sink Memorial Library at Mississippi State University, and a collection of Jones's work, "Knee-Deep In Mississippi," was published by Pelican Publishing in 1997.

Clay Jones
cjones@freelancestar.com

Kevin Kallaugher (KAL)

Kevin "KAL" Kallaugher is the editorial cartoonist for *The Baltimore Sun* and *The Economist* magazine of London.

After graduating from Harvard College with honors in 1977, Kallaugher embarked on a bicycle tour of the British Isles, where he joined the Brighton Basketball Club as a player and coach. In March 1978, *The Economist* recruited him to become their first resident cartoonist in its 145-year history.

Kallaugher returned to the U.S. in 1988 to join *The Sun* as its editorial cartoonist. He continues to draw three cartoons per week for *The Economist.* His work for *The Sun* and *The Economist* has appeared in more than 100 papers worldwide. His cartoons are distributed by Cartoonarts International and the New York Times Syndicate.

Kallaugher has won many awards for his work, including honors from the National Press Foundation in 2002, The Overseas Press Club of America in 2002 and 1999, the International Festival of Satire in Pisa, Italy, in 1996 and the Witty World International Cartoon Festival in Budapest, Hungary in 1990. He has published a collection of his *Economist* drawings and three collections of his *Baltimore Sun* cartoons.

Kallaugher is past President of the Association of American Editorial Cartoonists and has had one-man exhibitions in London, New York, Washington and Baltimore.

Kevin Kallaugher
kaltoons@comcast.net

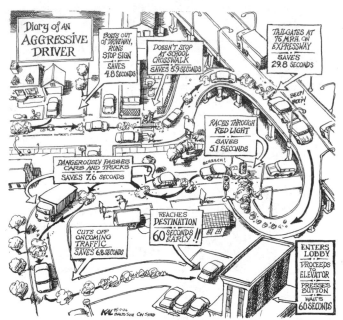

Mike Keefe

After a stretch in the Marine Corps and while working on a doctorate in mathematics at the University of Missouri at Kansas City, Mike Keefe began drawing editorial cartoons for the campus newspaper. The Vietnam War was winding down and Watergate was heating up. With material this rich, Keefe was fooled into believing that cartooning would always be easy. He gave up math and was hired by *The Denver Post*, where he still labors today.

His cartoons have appeared in *Time*, *Newsweek*, *U.S. News & World Report*, the *New Republic*, the *New York Times*, *Business Week*, the *Washington Post*, *George* and hundreds of other newspapers and magazines.

With varying degrees of success, Keefe has dabbled in cartoon strips, animation, books and screenplays.

Keefe served as president of the Association of American Editorial Cartoonists and is a former John S. Knight Fellow at Stanford University. Among other honors, he's won the National Headliner Award, Sigma Delta Chi Distinguished Service Award, The Best of the West Journalism contest, and the Fischetti Cartoon Competition. Keefe served as a Pulitzer Prize juror in 1997 and 1998.

Like most cartoonists he knows, Keefe plays in a rock band on the weekends.

Mike Keefe
www.InToon.com

Steve Kelley

For more than two decades, political cartoonist Steve Kelley has devoted his attention to public officials the way the radiator grille of a tractor-trailer might devote its attention to June bugs. He has delighted readers by consistently consigning office holders to the one fate they fear most: that of not being taken seriously.

Steve Kelley's cartoons are syndicated nationwide and appear frequently in *Newsweek, USA Today* and *The New York Times.* In 1999, he was one of three finalists for the Pulitzer Prize, and in 2001 won first-place awards from the California Newspaper Association, the Los Angeles Press Club and the National Headliner Awards.

In 2002, Kelley moved from San Diego to New Orleans, where he became the resident political cartoonist for *The Times-Picayune.*

"It's lifestyle whiplash." Kelley says. "I moved from San Diego, a city that is tidy and well governed, to the absolute epicenter of patronage and corruption. It's like I was married to a Junior Leaguer for two decades, then one morning woke up next to Dennis Rodman."

Not content with being funny in print, Kelley launched his second successful career in stand-up comedy. Now a veteran of seven appearances on "The Tonight Show," Kelley was featured on "The Late, Late Show with Tom Snyder" and has appeared at The Riviera, Harrah's and The Desert Inn in Las Vegas, as well as Carnegie Hall in New York.

Despite a dizzying schedule, Kelley gives much of his time and talent to charity. "Funny Money," which he co-created, provided funding for the San Diego Child Abuse Prevention Foundation for seven consecutive years. In 2001, he created "1000 Laughs for 1000 Smiles" to raise money for reconstructive surgery on cleft palates of children in Mexico.

Kelley is the father of a four-year-old son, Hayden, about whom he brags without regard to the listener's interest.

Steve Kelley
stevekelley@times-picayune.com

T. Brian Kelly

T. Brian Kelly, 43, is a freelance editorial cartoonist and humorous illustrator in Chicago, Illinois. He publishes local editorial cartoons in the *Daily Herald*, based in Arlington Heights, and his work has appeared in *The Washington Post National Edition*, the *San Francisco Chronicle*, *San Jose Mercury News*, *Oakland Tribune*, *Contra Costa Times*, the *Chicago Reader*, *Piedmont Post*, *ACLU-Northern California Journal*, *Berkeley Daily Planet*, *Oakland Urbanview*, *California Law Week*, *Hospitality Upgrade* and *Foreword Magazine*, among others.

He holds a BFA in painting from the University of Illinois at Urbana-Champaign, and has won regional, state and national awards for his cartoons.

His work was featured in the March 2002 edition of the American Society of Newspaper Editor's publication *The American Editor,* and is represented in the 2002 edition of "Best Editorial Cartoons of the Year" from Pelican Publishing.

Kelly devotes himself full-time to editorial and gag cartooning and part-time to screenwriting, while also being a full-time dad for his three children, ages 8, 6 and 4.

T. Brian Kelly
ragstandman@msn.com

[This cartoon and accompanying press helped fuel a vociferous public protest that derailed a backroom sweetheart deal to hand over the only public golf course in the city of Oakland, California, to a developer.]

Joe King

Joe King (a.k.a. "That Joe Guy") is the political cartoonist for the *Santa Monica Daily Press*. He is also a consultant and designer in the product and packaging for a wide variety of children's specialty items.

He is currently in production of several self-syndicated comics distributed worldwide under the banner of his publishing forge: www.FUNNYPAPERZ.com.

With more than 2,000,000 visitors to his website to date, King is being laughed at in more than 14 different countries. An honorary graduate of Platt College, he has been a guest speaker there, at the Pasadena Art Center School Of Design and at the Palos Verdes Art Institute. He is the founder of IMAGINE NATIONS, a global online community of amateur and professional cartoonists dedicated to freedom of thought.

He gets to play hooky more than the other dads, and his kids think the most bitchin' trophy atop his drawing board is the Elephant Key he won as a child in the *San Francisco Chronicle's* Junior Art Champion contest. (King was too young to enter, so he lied about his age — and won.)

Today King lies about any number of things except this: He can be found any evening with Angela, the love of his life, as they walk along the South Bay shore.

Joe King
Thatjoeguy@aol.com
www.FUNNYPAPERZ.com

THE GRASSHOPPER AND THE ANT (AND THE DONKEY AND THE ELEPHANT)

BUDGET SURPLUS!

WHOAH, DUDE! LET'S PARTY!

NO. WE MUST SAVE AND PREPARE FOR WHEN TIMES ARE HARSHER THAN THEY ARE NOW.

ACTUALLY, I HAVE TO GO ALONG WITH THE GRASSHOPPER.

OH, LET'S JUST GIVE IT ALL AWAY...

TAX CUTS FOR THE RICH

John Kovalic

USA Today has called John Kovalic a "hot pick." His work has appeared everywhere from *The New York Times*, the *Washington Post* and *Rolling Stone* to *Dragon* magazine. His editorial cartoons run in various newspapers around the world, while his other creations include the hit comic book *Dork Tower*, as well as *Dr. Blink: Superhero Shrink, Snapdragons*, and many other features.

Kovalic describes his editorial style as part of the "post-hatch" movement (see also: Joe Sharpnack; Scott Bateman). *Dork Tower* is a multi-Origins Award winner, while Kovalic's work on games like "Munchkin" and "Chez Geek" has also garnered multiple awards. In July 2003, Kovalic was inducted into the Academy of Adventure Gaming Arts and Design Hall of Fame, the first cartoonist to receive such an honor.

Kovalic is co-founder, co-owner and art director of Out Of The Box Games, producers of the million-selling, multi-award-winning "Apples To Apples" among many other games. He also created the "Whad'ya Know Party Game" in 2003. *[Full-disclosure time: Kovalic is also director of Dork Storm Press and the publisher of this book.]*

In his spare time, Kovalic searches for spare time.

John Kovalic
john@kovalic.com
www.dorktower.com

DORK TOWER by John Kovalic

EVERY NOW AND THEN WE READ ABOUT THE HOME OF THE FUTURE.

A HOME WHERE INTER-CONNECTIVITY AND WIRELESS TECHNOLOGY MEET INTELLIGENT APPLIANCES AND SMART GADGETS.

A HOME WHERE EVEN THE TOASTER HAS A PENTIUM IV.

A HOME, IN SHORT, WIRED FOR THE I-FUTURE!

VIRTUAL LAUNDRY

WELL, WE'D BE EXCITED...

Cat Food -a- tronic 2000

BUT I THINK WE ALL KNOW WHAT IT'LL **REALLY** BE LIKE...

THE SINK AND THE BIRDBATH ARE CONFLICTING, SO THEY BOTH CRASHED. THE TOILET HAS A 404 USER ERROR AND THE COFFEE POT'S DOWN WITH THE "CODE RED" WORM...

© 2001 SHETLAND PRODUCTIONS   JOHN@KOVALIC.COM HTTP://WWW.DORKTOWER.COM

PRESIDENCY

Don Landgren Jr.

Since 1982, Don Landgren Jr. has been the editorial cartoonist for *The Landmark,* a newspaper in central Massachusetts, where he mainly satirizes local issues — namely sewers, schools and water. He has also worked for the *Worcester Telegram & Gazette* since 1984, and is currently the newspaper's Chief Graphic Designer where he does page design, charts and "body-found-here maps."

His work has been reprinted in newspapers such as *The Boston Herald* and *Editorial Humor* as well as in magazines such as *Constitution, Public Citizen, Dog Fancy* and *Cat Fancy*, and in the annual anthology, "Best Editorial Cartoons of the Year."

Landgren's cartoons have won numerous awards from the National Newspaper Association, Suburban Newspapers of America, New England Press Association and the Massachusetts Press Association. He has been honored with awards from the Society of Newspaper Design, UPI New England and the New England Associated Press News Executives Association for his page designs in the *Worcester Telegram & Gazette.*

He has also received a t-shirt proclaiming him "Number One Dad."

He is a graduate of Anna Maria College. Don and his wife Jennifer have two daughters, Kyra and Bridget.

Don Landgren
don@donlandgren.com

GROWTH SPURT

Jim Larrick

Jim Larrick was born on the coast of North Carolina but grew up in Louisville, Kentucky. He holds degrees in journalism from Indiana University and business administration from the University of Kentucky. He also studied art at the University of Louisville.

Larrick began his newspaper career as a general-assignment reporter at *The Clarion-Ledger* in Jackson, Mississippi. He worked as a business reporter, business editor, entertainment editor and art director before turning his attention full time to cartooning. He joined the staff of *The Columbus Dispatch,* in Columbus, Ohio, in 1982.

Larrick is a Navy veteran and a past president of the Association of American Editorial Cartoonists.

Jim Larrick
34 S. Third St.
Columbus, OH 43215
jlarrick@dispatch.com

Vaughn Larson

Vaughn R. Larson has been the editorial cartoonist for *The Review* in Plymouth, Wisconsin, since 1993. His work also appears periodically in the *Wisconsin State Journal* in Madison.

In addition, he serves as *The Review's* news editor and chief page designer. Sometimes he takes photos, sometimes he writes sports stories, and sometimes he designs news graphics.

He also bags the newspapers for postal delivery during press runs.

In his secret identity, Larson is married to Wendy A. Larson and has four children. He is a section chief in a National Guard artillery battery in Wisconsin. He served in the 132nd Military History Detachment during Operation Desert Shield/Desert Storm. During this time, he freelanced as an Army artist for the Center for Military History. While in Saudi Arabia, Larson created the cartoon Strip "Sahara Smith," which detailed the exploits of a young private in the Gulf War for the VII Corps newspaper, the *Jayhawk*. Larson continued the strip for the Milwaukee Area Technical College newspaper *The Times,* for which he won a second-place award in the national College Media Advisors cartoon strip competition in 1992.

In 2000 he won honorable mention in the Fischetti editorial cartoon competition.

In 2001 he published his first, and so far only, cartoon book: "In the Wurst Way — A Collection of (Mostly) Sheboygan County and Wisconsin Cartoons."

Vaughn R. Larson
P.O. Box 317
Plymouth, WI 53073
www.plymouth-review/inkbombs

Mike Lester

Mike Lester has been an artist, illustrator and writer professionally for 20 years. He was born and raised in Atlanta, Georgia, and graduated with a degree in Graphic Design from the University of Georgia in 1977.

For over twenty years he has created images for the ad campaigns of major corporations and national magazines along with writing and illustrating numerous children's books, games and products.

He is also the editorial cartoonist for Georgia's *Rome News Tribune* and syndicated online through CagleCartoons.com.

Lester won the Designer of the Year award from Georgia Press Association in 2003.

He resides in downtown Rome, Georgia, with his gay cat.

Mike Lester
mlester101@comcast.net

Dick Locher

Dick Locher's ability to capture the absurdities of life through political cartooning resulted in his winning a Pulitzer Prize in 1983. His work also garnered the Sigma Delta Chi Award from the Society of Professional journalists, the John Fischetti Editorial Cartoon Award and the Overseas Press Club Award — twice.

Locher is nationally syndicated and his work appears regularly in *The Chicago Tribune*, as well as being reprinted in *Life, Time, Newsweek, U.S. News & World Report, Forbes, Playboy, National Review* and hundreds of newspapers throughout the world.

In March 1983, Locher took over drawing the "Dick Tracy" comic strip and was an assistant on the 1990 big-screen adaptation of the long-running strip. (In fact, Locher first worked on Dick Tracy as Chester Gould's assistant from 1957 to 1961.)

Locher studied art at the Chicago Academy of Fine Art and the Art Center of Los Angeles. He served in the U.S. Air Force as a pilot and aircraft designer, was president of his sales-promotion agency, and has been a painter, art director, sculptor and inventor.

Locher and his wife Mary live in the suburban Chicago area.

Dick Locher
tracyhq@aol.com

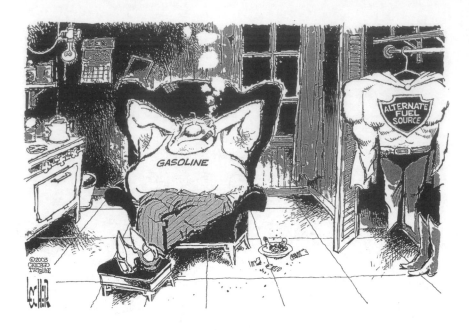

Andrew Long

Award-winning visual journalist Andrew Long has been an editorial cartoonist for several weekly newspapers in Arizona since 1999. He draws cartoons for the Freedom Communications-owned *Ahwatukee Foothills News*, *Scottsdale Views* and the *Chandler Connection*. He also works at *The Tribune*, a 100,000-circulation daily newspaper in Mesa, Arizona, and was the cartoonist for the *Gilbert Guardian* and *South Tempe Voice* until 2002.

Long lives in downtown Mesa with his very fat cat. When he isn't working, he can be found enjoying the Arizona outdoors.

Andrew Long
along@aztrib.com

Chan Lowe

Chan Lowe, editorial cartoonist for the *Sun-Sentinel* in Fort Lauderdale, Florida, was born in New York City in 1953, educated in New York, Los Angeles and England, and graduated from Williams College in 1975 with a degree in art history.

Lowe was employed as staff artist and editorial cartoonist for the *Shawnee News-Star* in Shawnee, Oklahoma, and served as editorial cartoonist for the *Oklahoma City Times* from 1978 to 1984. He has been with the *Sun-Sentinel* since 1984.

His cartoons are syndicated by Tribune Media Services and have won several awards, including the Green Eyeshade Award in 1992, and second place in the 1996 John Fischetti Competition. In 1990, he was a finalist for the Pulitzer Prize. Most recently, he was awarded The National Press Foundation's Berryman Award for excellence in editorial cartooning for the year 2000.

His cartoons have appeared on television and in numerous publications, including *Newsweek, the New York Times, the Washington Post,* and *USA Today*. He has also illustrated a humor book, "Are You A Newrotic."

In 1986, he was commissioned to design a poster by the Library of Congress, and a kinetic sculpture by Lowe was exhibited in 1997 at the National Gallery for Caricature and Cartoon Art in Washington, D.C. Lowe also spent a year studying at Stanford University as a John S. Knight Journalism Fellow in 1992-1993. His interests include history, woodworking and baroque music performance.

PROTECTING THE UNBORN ONLY GOES SO FAR.

Chan Lowe
954-356-4619
clowe@sun-sentinel.com

Mike Luckovich

After selling life insurance to make ends meet following his graduation from the University of Washington in 1982, Mike Luckovich landed his first cartooning job at the *Greenville News* in South Carolina. Nine months later, Luckovich was hired by *The Times-Picayune* in New Orleans, where he worked for four years before moving on to the *Atlanta Journal-Constitution* in 1989.

In 1989 he won the Overseas Press Club Award for Best Cartoons on Foreign Affairs, and in 1991, he was awarded the National Headliners award for editorial cartoonists. Luckovich was a runner-up for the Pulitzer Prize in 1987 and won journalism's biggest award in 1995.

His cartoons, distributed nationally by Creators Syndicate, appear in more than 350 daily publications including *The Washington Post, the Detroit News, Seattle Times, Los Angeles Times, the Chicago Tribune, the New York Times, Nashville Tennessean* and *the Houston Chronicle,* and are reprinted regularly in *Time* and *Newsweek.*

Luckovich and his wife Margo have four children. His hobbies include exercising and collecting unique ties.

Mike Luckovich
www.ajc.com

Ranan Lurie

Ranan Lurie, 71, was "imported" to the U.S. from his native Israel in 1968 by *Life* magazine to become its political cartoonist and cover artist for five years. The magazine sponsored his American citizenship.

After the demise of *Life*, he served for three years as political cartoonist and contributing editor for *Newsweek International,* and spent two years as senior analyst and political cartoonist for *U.S. News & World Report.*

Over the years, Lurie has worked as a cartoonist and analyst for the Japanese newspaper *Asahi Shimbun, The Times* of London, and West Germany's *Die Welt*, where he also did interviews. Since 1994, Lurie has produced a weekly cartoon page for *Time International* magazine. In 1997 he was invited by Europe's oldest paper, Switzerland's *Neue Zurcher Zeitung,* to launch its first political cartoon in 221 years. Since 2000, he has been regular political cartoonist for *Foreign Affairs.*

He is also the founder and editor of Cartoonews.com, The Current Events Educational Magazine, established in 1996.

He has been married for 43 years to his wife Tamar. They have four children: Rod (movie director and screen writer of "The Contender" and "The Last Castle"), Barak (lawyer and business executive), Daphne (psychologist), and Danielle (Stanford); and, three grandchildren: Hunter (13, Karate purple belt), Paige (11, Karate orange belt), and Samuel (Karate white diaper).

cartoonews@aol.com

"Freeze!!!"

"She likes me... she likes me not..."

Doug MacGregor

Doug MacGregor has been a cartoonist for *The News-Press* in Fort Myers, Florida, since 1988. He draws daily editorial cartoons and the Sunday feature "MacGregor's Boulevard." His comic feature "Sunny-Side Up" appears Wednesday and Thursday in the Lifestyles section and in "Tropicalia" on Sunday.

MacGregor is a native of Binghamton, New York, and a 1979 graduate of Syracuse University. He began his career as editorial cartoonist for the *Norwich Bulletin* in eastern Connecticut in 1980.

He has won several cartooning awards including the Best of Gannett, and top honors from the Society of Professional Journalists/Sunshine State and Florida Press Club.

When MacGregor isn't at his drawing board you can spot him at local schools, civic associations, libraries and hospitals talking to students and adults about cartooning, current events and the importance of reading a daily newspaper.

MacGregor also plays harmonica in a popular local blues band in the Fort Myers area.

Doug MacGregor
2442 Dr. MLK, Jr. Blvd
Fort Myers, FL 33901
239-335-0237
dmacgregor@news-press.com
www.news-press.com

Bruce MacKinnon

Bruce MacKinnon, a native of Antigonish, Nova Scotia, studied fine arts at Mount Allison University and graphic design at the Nova Scotia College of Art and Design. He started doing a weekly editorial cartoon for the *Halifax Chronicle-Herald* and *the Mail-Star* in 1985, working at home while raising his newborn daughter. He joined the *Herald* full-time in August of 1986, filling the void left by renowned cartoonist Bob Chambers.

In the time he has worked for the *Herald*, MacKinnon has been the recipient of eight Atlantic Journalism Awards for editorial cartooning, including one for Journalist of the Year. In both 1992 and 1993 he won the Canadian National Newspaper Award for editorial cartooning. In 1996 he was awarded an honorary doctorate by St. Mary's University for his work in the field of editorial cartooning.

In 1998 and 1999 he was again nominated for the National Newspaper Award for editorial cartooning, and in 2000 he was recognized with a lifetime achievement award from the Atlantic Journalism Awards. His work is syndicated through Artizans.

He lives in Halifax with his wife Peggy and their children, Robyn and Jamieson.

**Bruce MacKinnon
P.O. Box 610 Hfx., N.S.
Canada, B3J 2T2
bmackinnon@herald.ns.ca**

[Tony Blair, in the shadow of Winston Churchill.]

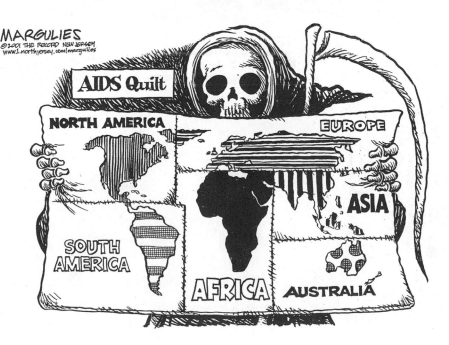

Jimmy Margulies

Jimmy Margulies joined *The Record* in Hackensack, New Jersey, as editorial cartoonist in 1990. His cartoons on New Jersey issues appear in newspapers throughout the state, and his work is distributed nationally to over 425 newspapers by King

Features/North America Syndicate. His work appears regularly in *Time, Newsweek, Business Week, the New York Times, the Washington Post, Los Angeles Times,* and *USA Today.*

In 1996, he won the National Headliner Award and the Fischetti Editorial Cartoon Competition. He also won the Deadline Club Award (given for the best in the New York City metro area) for cartoons done in 1998.

Margulies began his editorial career with Journal Newspapers of Maryland and Virginia. From 1984 to 1990, he was editorial cartoonist for *The Houston Post.* During that time he published his first collection of cartoons, "My Husband Is Not a Wimp!" In 1985, he won the Global Media Award of the Population Institute which included a two-week study tour of China, and in 1990, *Ultra* magazine named him to its list of Texans Who Made The Eighties.

A graduate of Carnegie Mellon University, he and his wife Martha, a teacher, have two children, Elana and David.

LARRY KING

Jimmy Margulies
150 River St.
Hackensack, NJ 07601
201-646-4468
jimmarg@aol.com

Gary Markstein

Since 1992, Gary Markstein has been an editorial cartoonist for *The Milwaukee Journal Sentinel* (previously *The Milwaukee Journal*). Prior to that, he was the editorial cartoonist for Tribune Newspapers in Mesa, Arizona. He received a Bachelor of Fine Arts degree from Arizona State University in 1982.

Markstein has received numerous cartoon awards. He won the 2000 and 2001 Global Media Award of Excellence, and the Family Planning Advocates Cartoon Award in 2002. He has received first place in the 1997 Fischetti Editorial Cartoon Competition, second place in the 1996 National Headliner Award, and third place in the 1996 National Press Foundation Berryman Awards, as well as several Milwaukee Press Club awards.

His cartoons are nationally syndicated by Copley News Service and have appeared in *Newsweek, the New York Times,* and *U.S. News & World Report.* In addition to editorial cartoons and illustrations, Markstein also draws a weekly cartoon on local and national sports topics.

Gary Markstein and his wife Beck have two young boys, Blake and Grant. For relaxation, he plays guitar in a rhythm and blues band.

Gary Markstein
333 W. State St.
Milwaukee, WI 53201
414-224-2360
gmarkstein@journalsentinel.com

Partial troop withdrawal

We Democrats deplore the President's use of military hardware for purely political motives.

SEN. ROBT BYRD

DUKAKIS

SHAMEFUL!

Jim McCloskey

Jim McCloskey has been the editorial cartoonist at *The News Leader* in Staunton, Virginia, for over 15 years. During that time he has been a consistent winner in the editorial-cartoon category at the Virginia Press Association's annual awards. In addition, the cartoonist has been honored by his newspaper company, garnering First Place in the "Best of Gannett" competition in 2001.

As a kid, he loved drawing and was a news junkie, even at an early age. After being exposed to editorial cartooning as a youth, he felt that this was a profession created just for him.

He draws six cartoons a week on local, state, national and world events. He has recently published a book of 150 of his best work titled, "Drawing Flak."

When McCloskey's not slinging ink around, his other passion is coaching his boys' soccer teams. He resides in the Shenandoah Valley of Virginia, with his wife Lori, three sons and one oversized cat.

Jim McCloskey
jmccloskey@newsleader.com

FUNNY HOW A JUVENILE WILL WANT TO BE TREATED AS AN ADULT UNTIL HE COMMITS MURDER.

Where are all the veterans, Daddy?

I DUNNO, SON.

KOREAN WAR VETS

W.W.II VETS

W.W.I VETS

Gary McCoy

Gary McCoy was born in 1962 — coincidentally, the same year that Gene Chandler released the hit song "Duke of Earl." You draw your own conclusions.

He grew up with three brothers, one being Glenn (who is also a cartoonist). McCoy started doing editorial cartoons in 1988 for *The Suburban Journals* of Greater St. Louis. His work has been distributed by Copley News Service, and reprinted in *The Washington Post.*

McCoy's comic strip, "That's My Dad," was syndicated with King Features in 1995. He has been a regular contributor to Playboy since 1997 and his work there has garnered him two consecutive nominations from the National Cartoonists Society for Best Gag Cartoonist of the Year.

He has freelanced for Anheuser Busch, Gibson Greetings, Disney and *Vivid* — a Romanian magazine. He has also worked as a full-time writer for his brother Glenn's nationally syndicated comic strip, "The Duplex."

In his free time, Gary McCoy enjoys exercising his right not to exercise.

Gary McCoy
908 Forest Ave.
Belleville, IL 62220
618-234-0082
gary@garymccoy.org
www.garymccoy.org

Glenn McCoy

Glenn McCoy was born in St. Louis, Missouri, and began drawing at age 4 under the tutelage of his grandfather and his older brother Gary. Weaned on "Peanuts" paperbacks, he acquired an early interest in cartooning and went on to draw for his grade school, high school and college newspapers. He graduated in 1988 from Southern Illinois University with a bachelor's degree in fine arts and graphic design.

McCoy soon landed a job as editorial cartoonist for the *Belleville News-Democrat* in his home town of Belleville, Illinois. In 1993 his comic strip, "The Duplex," was picked up by Universal Press Syndicate, and in 1999 Universal began syndicating his editorial cartoons.

His editorial cartoons have been reprinted in *The New York Times*, *USA Today* and *Newsweek*, and appear frequently on CNN. They have also been collected in two books, "Pot Shots" and "Pot Shots 2," both dealing with Bill Clinton's years in office. A collection of his "Duplex" cartoons has been published by Andrews McMeel Publishing.

In addition to his editorial cartoons, comic strip and magazine cartoons, McCoy has designed and written for several animation studios, including Dreamworks SKG, Film Roman, and Walt Disney TV and Feature Animation. His first children's book, "Penny Lee and Her TV," was published by Hyperion in 2002, and his second will be out for Christmas 2004.

Glenn and his wife Laura live in Belleville with their daughter Molly and dog Maggie.

Glenn McCoy
618-239-2669
glenn@glennmccoy.com

Rick McKee

From doodling pictures of the principal in class to skewering the president in the newspaper pages of America, Rick McKee has been cartooning all his life in one form or another.

McKee, 38, is one of the few conservative editorial cartoonists in a profession infested with liberals. A native of Tallahassee, Florida, he has been editorial cartoonist for Georgia's *The Augusta Chronicle* since January 1998.

His editorial cartoons are syndicated nationally by King Features/North American Syndicate, and have been reprinted in over 400 newspapers across the country as well as shown on CNN. His award-winning work has appeared in textbooks, newsletters and web sites around the world, as well as refrigerators and cubicle walls.

Rick McKee
3038 Sterling Rd.
Augusta, GA 30907
706-860-7424
rick.mckee@augustachronicle.com

"MARK MY WORDS, MILDRED!... IF WE DON'T GET SOME BETTER ELECTED OFFICIALS SOON, I SWEAR I'M GONNA GO DOWN to the POLLS and VOTE MYSELF!...."

"GOOD AFTERNOON, MA'AM.... I'M WITH THE U.S. CENSUS BUREAU.... DO YOU FEEL THAT GOVERNMENT IS MORE OR LESS INTRUSIVE THAN IT WAS A DECADE AGO?"

Salih Memecan

Salih Memecan draws a number of cartoons for *Sabah*, a major national Turkish newspaper, including a daily political cartoon strip,

"Bizimcity," on the front page; a daily comics cartoon strip, "Sizinkiler," on the back page; "Hayvanat," a daily animal cartoon for the third page; and twice-a-week foreign affair cartoons for the world page. The animated version of Bizimcity is seen daily on the prime-time news program on ATV.

His editorial cartoons have appeared in such major U.S. newspapers as *The Washington Post, the San Francisco Chronicle, the Baltimore Sun,* and *the Philadelphia Inquirer.*

Memecan was born in 1952 in Giresun, Turkey, and received his Ph.D. in architecture from the University of Pennsylvania in 1983 as a Fulbright scholar. He is married and has a son, Mehmet, and a daughter, Zeynep. He lives in Scarsdale, New York, from which he e-mails his cartoons to Istanbul daily.

**Salih Memecan
3 Forest Lane
Scarsdale NY 10583
914-713-0224
smemecan@bellatlantic.net
smemecan@sabah.com.tr**

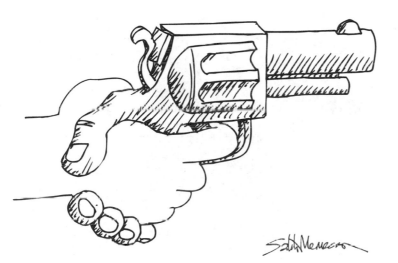

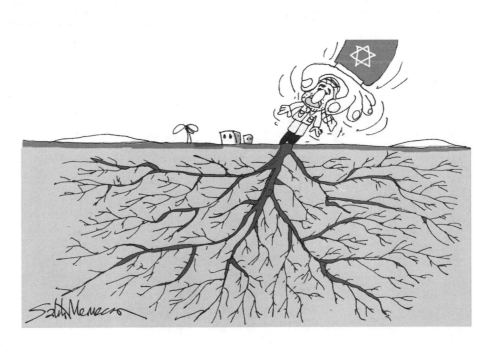

Tim Menees

Tim Menees was born in Seattle, and graduated from the University of Washington with a BA in political science. After serving in the Air Force, he worked as a reporter at the *Seattle Post-Intelligencer* and drew cartoons for the weekly *Bainbridge Island Review* in Washington (the inspiration for the newspaper in the novel "Snow Falling on Cedars").

Menees has been drawing cartoons at the *Pittsburgh Post-Gazette* since 1976. His work has appeared in the major national newspapers, including *The New York Times* and *The Washington Post*, in national news magazines and on network TV. His work has placed second in the John Fischetti Editorial Cartoon Competition, won the National Newspaper Association award for weekly cartoons, and received several regional awards.

He has drawn three syndicated comic strips and now writes and draws a weekly satire column for the paper. Two one-act plays of his have won a full production and a seated reading in national competition.

Tim Menees is married, and has a son and a daughter and a cat. He also paints, and plays piano and accordion in a blues-zydeco band.

Tim Menees
tmenees@post-gazette.com

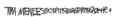

I SEE "NO PREDICTIONS UNTIL ALL PRECINCTS ARE IN."

Deb Milbrath

Deb Milbrath was born and raised in cheese-head country — a.k.a. Wisconsin. Jobs in retail advertising later transplanted her to Minneapolis, New York City, Washington D.C., and finally Atlanta, where she discovered the life of a freelance designer, illustrator and editorial cartoonist.

Her work has been featured in the *Atlanta Journal-Constitution, New York Daily News,* CNN Headline News and lots of other publications too insignificant to mention.

Deb Milbrath
dmilbrath@mindspring.com
www.milbrathdraws.com

TODAY MILLIONS OF AMERICANS RETURN FROM THE LABOR DAY HOLIDAY RELAXED AND READY TO RESUME THEIR JOB SEARCH.

What Stinks?

I DON'T SMELL ANYTHING.

DEFICIT

TONIGHT'S GUEST IS TV PSYCHIC JOHN EDWARDS WHO WILL ATTEMPT TO CONTACT THE SPIRIT OF MAJOR GENERAL DWIGHT D. EISENHOWER TO GET HIS TAKE ON THE WAR AGAINST IRAQ.

LARRY KING LIVE

USA

Geoffrey Moss

During the Watergate Scandal, Geoffrey Moss' "noir" visual commentary was recognized with a Pulitzer nomination and the publication of the book, "The Art and Politics of Geoffrey Moss," with a foreword by Dan Rather.

As the first op-ed artist nationally syndicated without captions, Moss doggedly refuses traditionalism. His content is not based on assignment, but drawn as a sole reaction to the issues of the day, as any political cartoonist would. Literally working "outside the box," Moss has helped changed the look of national opinion pages with his commentary.

Moss received a BA from the University of Vermont, and a BFA and MFA from Yale School of Art and Architecture. He worked for *The Washington Post* during the early 1970s, before joining the Washington Post Writers Group Syndicate as a founding member. He is now represented by Creators Syndicate.

In 2001, Moss was nominated for a Pulitzer for his material on 9/11, and his work has been exhibited in group shows at the Smithsonian Institution in Washington D.C., and the Andy Warhol Museum in Pittsburgh, Pennsylvania.

In 2002, Simon & Schuster published Moss' book of photography and interviews, "The Biker Code."

Geoffrey Moss
mossprince@aol.com

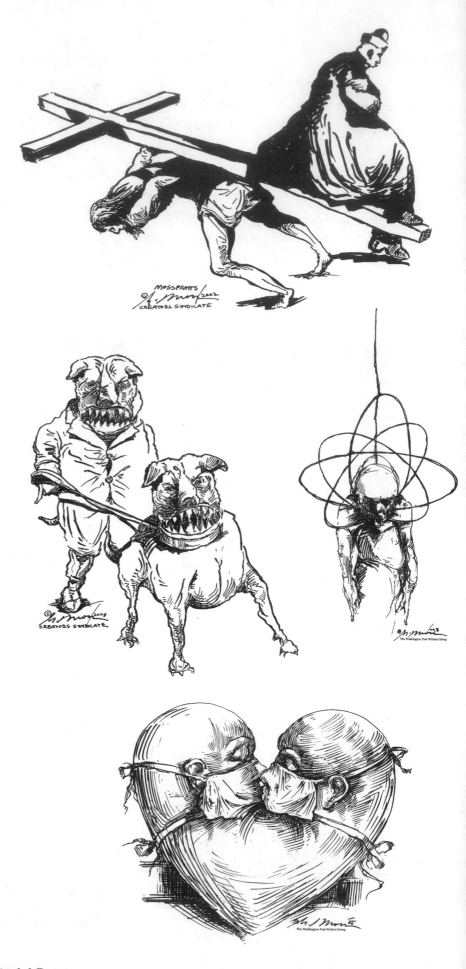

THE ELECTRONIC BABY SITTER

Ricky Nobile

Ricky Nobile is a native of Moorhead, Mississippi who attended Mississippi Delta Community College and the University of Southern Mississippi. He has syndicated editorial cartoons to Mississippi newspapers since 1971 and has been editorial cartoonist for the *Mississippi Business Journal* since 1997. He also draws a weekly editorial cartoon as well as sports cartoons for the *Hattiesburg American*. His cartoons have been published in "Best Editorial Cartoons of the Year," *Harvard Political Review* and other books and magazines.

One of Nobile's favorite activities is attending University of Southern Mississippi athletic events with family and friends. He created a Southern Miss Golden Eagle coloring book that sells in the USM Bookstore and other retail outlets in the area. It received such great response that he has since created several other specialty books for other organizations in the Hattiesburg area.

Nobile, his wife Mary, daughter Emily and nephew James Shelton live in Hattiesburg, Mississippi.

Ricky Nobile
P.O. Box 16064
Hattiesburg, MS 39404
601-583-0649
nobilericky@aol.com

THAT TIME OF THE YEAR

FLOOD WARNING

Paul Nowak

Paul Nowak has been working as a cartoonist since 1993, when he began a weekly strip in an English-language paper in Japan that ran for five years. Since 1999, his work has been published online at CNSNews.com, ConsumerFreedom.com, and other political sites. Print has been a bit tougher to break into, but Nowak was published by Scripps Howard News Service from 2001 to 2003.

His current clients include *MARINES* magazine, the American Legislative Exchange Council newsletter and an occasional book. He lives in Chicago and always welcomes freelance work requests.

Paul Nowak
7312 N. Greenview Ave.
Chicago, IL 60626
(773) 764-6286
usernowak@aol.com

FRIENDLY FIRE

Patrick O'Connor

Patrick O'Connor is the editorial cartoonist at the *Los Angeles Daily News*.

Born in March 1977 in Dublin, Virginia, O'Connor has been drawing ever since he

can remember. Having lived in Virginia, Pennsylvania, Georgia and Ohio, and attended six different schools in his formative years, he understands the power of ridicule. A graduate in art and journalism from Kent State University, O'Connor began his career at the *Daily Kent Stater*, the *Record-Courier* of Ravenna, Ohio, and *the Washington Times*.

His cartoons are currently published in Southern California's *Long Beach Press Telegram, Pasadena Star News, San Bernardino County Sun, San Gabriel Tribune* and *the Redlands Daily Facts*.

O'Connor is the winner of the John Locher Memorial Award in 1998 and the Society of Professional Journalists National Mark of Excellence Award in 1999. He was also honored by the Associated Press of Ohio in 2000 and the Los Angeles Press Club in 2002.

When not drawing political cartoons, O'Connor can be found life drawing, painting, sculpting, playing the guitar or banjo, and reading. He and his wife Laura live in Los Angeles with their two cats.

Patrick O'Conner
21221 Oxnard St.
Woodland Hills, CA 91367
818-713-3650
patrick.oconner@dailynews.com

Jack Ohman

Jack Ohman has been editorial cartoonist for *The Oregonian* in Portland, Oregon, since 1983. His work is syndicated to 300 newspapers in the United States and abroad by Tribune Media Services, and he is the author of eight books.

Previously, Ohman worked at the *Columbus Dispatch* and the *Detroit Free Press.* He attended the University of Minnesota from 1978 to 1981, and worked as the cartoonist for the *Minnesota Daily.* At 19, he was the youngest cartoonist ever to be nationally syndicated.

Ohman won the 1980 Sigma Delta Chi Mark of Excellence Award for best college editorial cartoon, the 1995 Overseas Press Club Award, and the 2002 National Headliners Award. From 1994 to 1999, Ohman drew the comic strip "Mixed Media," also syndicated by Tribune Media Services, which appeared in 175 newspapers.

Ohman has a bachelor's degree in History from the University Honors Program at Portland State University. He is married to Janice Dunham Ohman and they have three children.

Jack Ohman
jackohman@news.oregonian.com

Michael Osbun

After being employed as a corporate advertising artist in New Jersey for a number of years, Michael Osbun decided to relocate to central Florida with his wife Jackie, where he worked as an instructor of comic art at the Disney Institute.

Osbun began freelancing editorial cartoons for the *Citrus County Chronicle* and two weekly publications in the area, and has since won six Florida Press Awards. He also provides editorial illustrations for distribution by Tribune Media Services and writes gags for syndicated comic strips.

Osbun's free time is spent on jogging, reading, having fun helping his wife with environmental causes and raising three dogs that are always a great source of comic inspiration.

Michael Osbun
Osbun@lcia.com

Frank Page

Frank Page began cartooning at an early age doing a comic strip for *The Knight Times*, his high school newspaper. Upon graduation in 1993, he enrolled at the State University of New York at Albany to pursue a degree in philosophy. While at Albany, he did a cartoon panel for the university paper *The ASP*.

After two years at SUNY Albany, Page transferred to Cazenovia College. He did a weekly strip for the college's newspaper *The QUAD* called "spare parts." He graduated in 1997 with a BFA in illustration, Magna Cum Laude. Immediately after graduation, Page got a job in the production department at the *Rome Daily Sentinel* in New York.

In 1999, Page was given the opportunity to do a weekly editorial cartoon – which eventually became five-a-week. Page won the Best Cartoon Award from the Syracuse Press Club three years in a row, and a 2000 Honorable Mention and a 2003 third place prize from the National Newspaper Association.

In 2001, Page published his first collection of cartoons "On the Page." His cartoons are also featured in the National Head Start Association's quarterly publication *Children and Families*.

Frank Page
333 W. Dominick St.
Rome, NY 13440
315-337-4000
fpage@ny.com

Gus Papoutsis

Gus Papoutsis specializes in the print and film animation market. He has worked as an animator for Disney, MGM, Marvel and other companies. In 2001, he expanded his market to include editorial cartooning, which he currently distributes through Gustoons Syndicate. He co-produced a strip titled "Digitizing Donnie" and has provided illustrations for several publications including *The Globe and Mail* and *The Canadian Forum.*

Papoutsis attended Sheridan College's Classical Animation program, completed a certificate from the Institute of Canadian Advertising, and is presently in completion of an honours degree from the University of Toronto.

In addition to his professional activities, Papoutsis appears as a visiting artist to Toronto elementary schools, and is currently the vice-president for the At-large chapter of the Graphic Artists Guild. He has been profiled in the Salon, in France, in celebration of Canada's Editorial Cartoonists (www.st-just.com).

Gus Papoutsis
416-833-9237
gusp@look.ca

Jeff Parker

Jeff Parker grew up with rockets on Florida's Space Coast. He has been editorial cartoonist for *Florida Today* in his hometown of Melbourne since 1992. Parker also assists Dean Young and Denis Lebrun with creating "Blondie," as well as helping Mike Peters with his strip "Mother Goose & Grimm."

Parker's work has been recognized with awards from Gannett News Service, the Society of Professional Journalists and the Florida Press Association. He was nominated by the National Cartoonists Society for the Reuben Category Award for Editorial Cartooning in 1997, 1998 and 2001.

His cartoons are distributed online by Caglecartoons.com.

Jeff Parker
parkertoons@reuben.org

THE BLIND DEMOCRATS AND THE ELEPHANT

DROWNING IN A SEA OF FORMS...

SW Parra

SW Parra is a staff artist and contributing editorial cartoonist for *The Fresno Bee* in California.

Drawing has been a part of Parra's life for as long as he can remember; politics and social issues have been recurring themes. In second grade, while most "normal" children were drawing rockets, flowers or animals, he was creating caricatures of President Richard M. Nixon.

In 1988 and 1989, his cartoons placed first during the California Intercollegiate Press Association's annual journalism competition.

After going to college at Cal State Fullerton, Parra worked for *The Los Angeles Times* in Orange County, drawing letters-to-the-editor artwork, while serving as the editorial cartoonist for the *Irvine World News* and *The Tustin Weekly*. He was hired as a staff artist by *The Press-Enterprise* in Riverside, California, and in 1991, *The Fresno Bee* recruited him to work as a news artist and art director.

His work also appears in *The Student Press Law Center Report* and was recognized by the California Newspapers Publishers Association in 2000.

SW Parra is a member of the National Association of Hispanic Journalists and Society of News Design.

"Let's see who's got more pull, me or you ..."

S.W. Parra
559-441-6293
swparra@fresnobee.com

Henry Payne

Henry Payne is an editorial cartoonist for *The Detroit News* and a freelance writer.

Payne produces ten cartoons a week which are syndicated to 60 papers worldwide by United Features. His cartoons are also reprinted in *The New York Times*, *USA Today* and *National Review*. He has been a runner-up for both the Pulitzer and Mencken awards.

Payne also writes and draws a weekly "cartoon column" called "Payne & Ink" and contributes regular sports and auto cartoons to the *The Detroit News'* sports and business pages.

Payne has reported stories for *The Wall Street Journal*, the *Weekly Standard* magazine, *National Review*, *Reason*, *Rocky Mountain News*, the *Pittsburgh Post-Gazette*, Scripps Howard News Service and numerous newspapers around the country.

In 2002 he published his first book, "Payne & Ink: The Cartoons and Commentary of Henry Payne, 2000-2001." Payne was also creator of the now-defunct comic strip, "Hub & Axel."

Payne received a degree in history from Princeton University in 1984 and began his newspaper career with the *Charleston Daily Mail* in West Virginia. He is an active race car driver, and tennis and squash player. He lives with his wife and two children in Bloomfield Hills, Michigan.

Henry Payne
www.HenryPayne.com

"SUV or non-SUV?"

"More coal?! No, man! . . . Wind power!"

"Kim Jong Il's hairstyle is really starting to freak my out!"

Donald Peoples

Donald E. Peoples came into the world in Akron, Ohio, on August 16, 1960. As a child, he loved drawing and coloring with crayons; he also loves to draw and color as an adult, only the supplies are a bit more expensive.

Peoples earned a BFA degree in graphic design from the University of Akron, and since 1989 he has been a graphic artist at the Akron-Summit County Public Library.

He has shown his "Cool Cartoons & Groovy Graphics" presentation at libraries and schools throughout northeast Ohio, and illustrated "The ABCs of Akron & Summit County Coloring & Activity Book."

His work has also graced the pages of the magazine *Comic Edge; Pacific*, the Sunday magazine of the *Seattle Times* newspaper; the *Clarke County Democrat* in Alabama; and the *Cleveland Monitor* newspaper.

His cartoons have been selected for the book, "So What If They Can't Take a Joke!" and received honorable mentions in 2000 and 2001 in the Homer Davenport Days International Cartoon Contest.

When Peoples is away from the computer and drawing table, he enjoys bowling, golf and supporting the arts.

Donald Peoples
1091 Packard Dr.
Akron, OH 44320
330-867-0651
depgraphic@aol.com

Joel Pett

Joel Pett, winner of the 2000 Pulitzer Prize for editorial cartooning, has been at Kentucky's *Lexington Herald-Leader* since 1984. His cartoons have appeared in hundreds of newspapers and magazines nationwide, including *The Washington Post, the New York Times, Los Angeles Times,* and *the Chicago Tribune.* He is a regular contributor to *USA Today,* and the educational journal *Phi Delta Kappan.* He is a past president of the Association of American Editorial Cartoonists.

Pett is also the winner of the 1999 Robert F. Kennedy Journalism Award for cartoons highlighting the plight of the disadvantaged, and the 1995 Global Media Award for cartoons on population issues. Pett's cartoons are available in five paperback editions, the most recent being "Thinking Inside the Box."

Having observed life in over twenty-five countries, from his boyhood home in Nigeria, down the Amazon, to Red Square, Tiananmen Square and beyond, Pett sums up his philosophy simply: "Hello, God?… We could use some help down here…"

He is proudest of a college intramural golf title, and of shutting out a University of Kentucky basketball player in a celebrity game of HORSE.

His list of embarrassments is endless.

Joel Pett
jpett@herald-leader.com
www.kentucky.com/mld/kentucky/

AFTER I'VE BEEN DRIVING THE KIDS AROUND IN THE MINIVAN A LOT,

I CAN ONLY FOCUS ON WHAT'S RIGHT AHEAD, AND EVERYTHING ELSE GETS DARK...

ALMOST LIKE DRIVING UNDERGROUND.

AH, I SEE.... CARPOOL TUNNEL SYNDROME.

Hap Pitkin

Hap Pitkin lapsed into editorial cartooning in 2000, after chequered careers as a soap

salesman, diplomat, human rights advocate, university administrator, career counselor and nonprofit director. He was drawn to cartooning because it provided a chance to get paid for exactly the kinds of

ideas that got him into trouble in his other jobs. And, er ... to work for world peace.

His cartoons appear in the *Boulder Daily Camera, the Longmont Times-Call* and other regional publications, and have been reprinted in "Best Editorial Cartoons of the Year."

He lives in Boulder, Colorado, with his wife and two daughters, who have nearly as many pets as they do basketballs, if you can imagine that.

Hap Pitkin
303-499-1634
hapandthem@aol.com

REMIND ME, KARL ... ARE WE HOPING THE WAR DISTRACTS THEM FROM THE ECONOMY, OR IS IT THE OTHER WAY AROUND?

ROVE

YEP, I GOT THIS THING PRETTY MUCH UNDER CONTROL HERE.

IRAQ

Academic Salaries in Colorado: A Modest Comparison.

ABOUT $ 22,000 = ONE PRESCHOOL TEACHER.

2 PRESCHOOL TEACHERS = 1 PUBLIC SCHOOL TEACHER.

2 PUBLIC SCHOOL TEACHERS = 1 CU FULL PROFESSOR.

14 CU FULL PROFESSORS = 1 CU HEAD FOOTBALL COACH.*

(Includes retention bonuses. CU pays 47% of the coach's total salary.)

Attack of the Political Cartoonists 107

Bruce Plante

Bruce Plante has been cartooning in Chattanooga, Tennessee, since 1985 for the *Chattanooga Times* and *Chattanooga Free Press.* His cartoons have been shown on CNN and CBS, and reprinted in *The New York Times, the Washington Post, USA Today, Newsweek, Newsweek Europe, Newsweek Japan, Sports Illustrated, Discover,* college and high school textbooks, and even the Iowa Achievement Test.

His editorial cartoons are syndicated by Universal Press Syndicate in more than 80 newspapers nationwide. He is also the creator of the outdoor comic panel "Born Lucky," which is also syndicated nationally by Universal Press Syndicate

He won the Fischetti Award in 2003. His other honors include the 2002 Tennessee Education Association School Bell Award, the Associated Press Public Service Award and the Silver Gavel from the American Bar Association. (He also won Showtime's Funniest Person in America Contest … but only in Chattanooga.)

Plante was the president of the Association of American Editorial Cartoonists in 2002-2003.

Plante has coached Little League baseball and football for 16 years. He and wife Betsy recently celebrated their 26th wedding anniversary.

Bruce Plante
P.O. Box 1447
Chattanooga, TN 37401
bplante@timesfreepress.com

Dwane Powell

Dwane Powell has been editorial cartoonist for *The News & Observer* in Raleigh, North Carolina, since 1975.

While in college at the University of Arkansas he had a reputation as a prolific doodler, leaving stacks of napkin drawings all around campus. The editor of the school newspaper coaxed Powell to try his hand at political cartoons, and his first attempt was picked up and published on the op-ed page of the statewide *Arkansas Gazette*.

Powell turned the weekly exposure the *Gazette* had afforded him into a full-time job as a reporter/cartoonist/photographer/flunkie at the *Hot Springs Sentinel Record*.

After a stint at the *San Antonio Light* as a staff artist and editorial cartoonist, his next stop was a full-time cartoonist gig at the *Cincinnati Enquirer*, until ideological differences prompted a move back south to the more liberal *News & Observer*.

Powell's work is carried by Creators Syndicate and has won the Overseas Press Club Citation for Excellence in Cartooning, and the National Headliners Club award.

Dwane Powell
215 S. McDowell St.
Raleigh, NC 27602
dpowell@nando.com

Milt Priggee

Milt Priggee was born in July 1953 in Anchorage, Alaska. He grew up in the Chicago area, where both of his parents were artists. After graduating from Adams State College with a major in fine arts, Priggee met his mentor, Pulitzer Prize-winning cartoonist John Fischetti of the *Chicago Sun-Times*. Fischetti helped Priggee start freelancing, and his work appeared in *The Chicago Daily News, Sun-Times* and *Chicago Tribune*.

Beginning in 1978, Priggee was the first regular cartoonist for the weekly *Crain's Chicago Business*. Later, he was staff editorial cartoonist with the *Journal-Herald* in Dayton, Ohio, from 1982 to 1986. Priggee created editorial cartoons for *The Spokesman-Review* in Spokane, Washington, from February 1987 to August of 2000. Currently he is freelancing animated and print editorial cartoons from his web site in northwest Washington State.

His work has been reprinted in *Time, Newsweek, U.S. News & World Report, the New York Times, the Washington Post* and *USA Today*.

Priggee has won awards from the Associated Press Society of Ohio, National Newspaper Association, Overseas Press Club, the Small Business Foundation of America, Pacific Northwest Journalists, Inland Northwest Society of Professional Journalists, Utah-Idaho-Spokane AP, and won the Fischetti Editorial Cartoon contest, Mencken Award, and the first Iran Internet Cartoon contest.

A past president of the Association of American Editorial Cartoonists, Priggee initiated the Association's Golden Spike award, given annually to the AAEC member with the best "killed cartoon."

Milt is married to Janet, his soul mate, and is the stepfather to Jason, 25, Jennifer, 23, and the father of Sarah, 21, and Eric, 19.

Milt Priggee
www.miltpriggee.com

"WE'D HAVE A LOT MORE MONEY IF OUR ROCKETS BLEW STUFF UP"

IT'S ALL OVER BUT THE CRYING...

Cindy Procious

Cindy Procious was born in November 1965 in Morristown, New Jersey, and moved to Huntsville, Alabama, when she was 4. Her

parents divorced when she was 8 years old, and she split time between her father's home in Huntsville and wherever the wind blew her mother.

She attended the University of Alabama in Huntsville for three years as an art major, until her higher education goals were thwarted by cruel economic realities.

Over the ensuing years, Procious held many jobs in the graphic arts field, and in August of 1998 she began lobbying *The Huntsville Times* to publish her work. After a deluge of several dozen cartoons crossed the editor's desk, he finally succumbed and agreed to publish her local and state cartoons.

Procious was named by the Society for Professional Journalists as a finalist for the 2000 Green Eyeshade Award for editorial cartooning after less than two years of cartooning experience.

Procious lives and works in Boston, Massachusetts. She is married to Clay Bennett, the editorial cartoonist for the *Christian Science Monitor*, and has three children, Matt, Ben and Sarah, none of whom yet draw for a newspaper.

Cindy Procious
cprocious@mac.com

IF THERE IS ANYONE PRESENT WHO CAN SHOW JUST CAUSE WHY THESE TWO SHOULD NOT BE JOINED, SPEAK NOW OR FOREVER HOLD YOUR PEACE.

Catch anything, Dear?

...Dysentery.

NEWS
FLINT RIVER CONTAMINATED W/ FECAL COLIFORM BACTERIA

Ted Rall

Cartoonist and writer Ted Rall was born in 1963 in Cambridge, Massachusetts, and raised in Kettering, Ohio. He majored in history and physics at Columbia University, where he drew cartoons for the *Columbia Daily Spectator.*

Rall signed on with Chronicle Features in 1991 and moved to Universal Press Syndicate in 1996. His cartoons now appear in more than 140 publications, including the *Philadelphia Daily News,*

Aspen Times, Hartford Advocate, Newark Star-Ledger, Los Angeles Times, Wilmington News-Journal, San Diego Reader, the Village Voice, the (Harrisburg) Patriot-News, Las Vegas Review Journal,
Washington City Paper, Sacramento News & Review, San Jose Mercury-News, Lexington Herald-Leader and *the New York Times.*

Rall has published ten books of his material, including three collections of his editorial cartoons: "Waking Up In America" in 1992, "All The Rules Have Changed" in 1995 and "Search and Destroy" in 2001. He also edited two collections of alternative cartoonists: "Attitude: The New Subversive Political Cartoonists," and "Attitude2: The New Subversive Alternative Cartoonists."

"To Afghanistan and Back," a graphic travelogue chronicling Rall's harrowing experiences covering the 2001 war, was a bestseller picked as a Best Book of the Year by the American Library Association.

His cartoons were awarded the 1998 Deadline Club Award by the Society of Professional Journalists, and received first place in both the 1995 and 2000 Robert F. Kennedy Journalism Awards.

Ted Rall lives in Manhattan with his wife Judy Chang, son Eric and cat Indy.

Ted Rall
chet@rall.com
www.rall.com

NEWS FLASH: IT DOESN'T WORK THIS WAY.

David Reddick

Since 1998, David Reddick has been the full-time staff editorial cartoonist and newsroom artist for *The Herald Bulletin* in Anderson, Indiana.

His editorial cartoons and daily single-panel cartoon "Reddick's Rhetoric" are distributed nationwide by CNHI News Service, and worldwide by Artizans Syndicate. His first book collects more than 200 of his cartoons and features a forward by Jim Davis, creator of Garfield.

Reddick's paintings and original cartoons have been featured in exhibitions and one-man shows in galleries and museums nationwide, and he has had cartoons appear in a gallery exhibition in Carquefou, France.

Reddick has won a number of awards from the Hoosier State Press Association, including first place for best illustration in 1999 and 2002, and first place for best editorial cartoonist in 2001. He also took first place in the 1998 National Thomson Annual Editorial Award of Excellence for best editorial cartoons and illustration.

David Reddick
reddickulous@aol.com

Mikhaela Reid

Mikhaela B. Reid is a 24-year-old political cartoonist for the *Boston Phoenix*. Her work has also appeared in *Funny Times, Bay Windows* and other publications. Reid was born in Lowell, Massachusetts, where she attended Lowell High School and was president of its Gay/Straight Alliance. More recently she graduated from Harvard, where she studied anthropology and photography, and drew cartoons for *The Harvard Crimson*.

Reid currently lives in Brooklyn and works as an information designer. She loves: her family, sewing, steamed dumplings and science fiction. She loathes with every fiber of her being: George W. Bush and his co-conspirators.

[Above, Reid drew this cartoon after would-be governor Mitt Romney ran a series of insubstantial campaign ads aimed at women voters, one that featured a story about Romney taking his wife to the prom and shots of a topless Romney frolicking in the water at the beach with his sons, or working different jobs for a day — hot dog vendor, construction worker, etc.]

Mikhaela Reid
toons@mikhaela.net
www.mikhaela.net

RELAX, THE LIBERTARIAN PARTY ASSURES ME THAT I'M NOT SHOOTING MYSELF IN THE FOOT.

MASSACHUSETTS

[Despite a budget crisis and massive deficit, the Libertarian Party places a proposal on the state ballot that would eliminate Massachusetts' income tax.]

Bob Rich

Bob Rich is the staff illustrator and editorial cartoonist for *The Republican* in Springfield, Massachusetts.

Rich was born in Escanaba, Michigan, and raised in Piqua, Ohio. Prior to working for *The Republican,* he was the art director and editorial cartoonist at the *Connecticut Post* in Bridgeport, Connecticut, for 10 years. In 1991 he worked for the now defunct *Knoxville Journal* in Tennessee. He has also been the editorial cartoonist for the *New Haven Register* in Connecticut and a staff artist for the *Knoxville News-Sentinel*.

A winner of numerous awards for his work, Rich has been honored by the Connecticut Chapter of SPJ and UPI. He received honorable mentions in the 1984 and 1985 John Fishcetti Editorial Cartoon Competition and the 1983 Charles M. Schulz Award for Promising Cartoonists.

Rich lives in Connecticut with his wife, Gloria. They have one son, Robert, and two cats.

Bob Rich
1860 Main St.
Springfield, MA 01103
brich@repub.com

PINK SLIPS?

THE BLIZZARD OF 2003

THE MASSACHUSETTS PRIMER

THE DOGGY GOES — BOW WOW

THE KITTY GOES — MEOW

...AND THE CHAINSAW GOES — VROOM! Mitt Mitt Mitt...

STATE EDUCATION BUDGET

[Massachusetts Governor Mitt Romney cuts the state education budget.]

Jon Richards

Jon Richards has been doing editorial cartoons in the capital city of Santa Fe, New Mexico, since 1988.

His cartoons currently appear biweekly in the *Albuquerque Journal North.* In the past they have been seen in the *Santa Fe New Mexican,* the *Santa Fe Reporter,* and the *Oklahoma City Gazette,* and were distributed regionally by the Sunmount Syndicate. He has been editorial cartoonist for Theodore Kheel's *Earth Summit Times* and the New York City press corps's *Inner Circle.* For a period in the mid-1990s, he and former National Security Council staffer Roger Morris collaborated on a column/cartoon package called "Lines Drawn."

Richards has engaged in a variety of other careers: novelist, screenwriter, movie critic, actor, television courtroom artist, advertising copywriter, songwriter, subtitlist and writer/director of film dubbing. His movie reviews appear weekly in the *Santa Fe New Mexican's Pasatiempo* and on various online sites including Rotten Tomatoes.

His novels include "The Whitmarsh Chronicles," a generational trilogy set against the background of the American labor movement; "Tularosa and Cherokee Bill," historical fiction with Western settings; and "Santa Fe," a novel of greed and growth in the stylish capital of New Mexico.

Jon Richards
www.rottentomatoes.com/
author-2779/

Mike Ritter

Since 1992, Mike Ritter has been the editorial cartoonist for Arizona's second largest paper, the East Valley/Scottsdale *Tribune* in Phoenix, Arizona.

Previously, he served as cartoonist for the *Scottsdale Progress,* which merged with *The Tribune* in 1993.

Ritter is a 1990 graduate of Arizona State University with a degree in history. During his four years at ASU's *State Press,* he received 10 Gold Circle Awards from Columbia University's Scholastic Press Association, including two first-place awards in 1990, in the editorial cartoon and comic strip categories.

He has been honored by the Suburban Newspapers of America and received the Arizona Press Club's first-place award for cartooning in 1993, 1995, 1996 and 2000. His cartoons won first-place honors in the Best of the West journalism contest in 2001 and 2003. In 1999 Ritter received the Thomson newspaper chain's highest award for illustration and a Freedom of Information Award from the Arizona Newspaper Association.

His work appears regularly in "Best Editorial Cartoons of the Year," and he has done illustrations for *USA Today* and *The New York Times Magazine.*

Ritter is a charter member in the Arizona Chapter of the National Lesbian & Gay Journalists Association, and spent 2003-2004 as president of the Association of American Editorial Cartoonists.

Ritter harbors a bizarre fascination with the movies of Bing Crosby and Bob Hope and has an encyclopedic knowledge of songs from the 1930s and '40s, which he sings relentlessly. He is also single. Coincidence?

Mike Ritter
mikerittermail@aol.com
www.mikeritter.com

Attack of the Political Cartoonists 117

Vance Rodewalt

Vance Rodewalt was born in 1946 in Alberta, Canada, to a horse-ranching family. After being bit and kicked and made to shovel out "way too many stinky stalls," he decided to pursue a career in art when he won a scholarship.

Rodewalt has done advertising and gag cartoons, freelanced to Marvel Comics and drawn editorial cartoons for the *Calgary Herald.* He also drew an internationally syndicated strip called "Chubb and Chauncey."

Rodewalt lives with his wife, a former champion figure skater, and their two boys in Calgary.

He also shoots a mean game of pool

Vance Rodewalt
rodewaltv@theherald.southam.ca

Thanksgiving at the Governor's Mansion

[*Under Governor Mike Easley, a former prosecutor, the state of North Carolina set a modern-day record for executions in 2003.*]

[*A tip of the hat to Al Hirschfeld, who died on the eve of the Iraq war.*]

V. Cullum Rogers

V. Cullum Rogers has been editorial cartoonist for *The Independent Weekly* in Durham, North Carolina, since 1997.

Born in 1949 in Bennettsville, South Carolina, he received a B.A. in english from Davidson College and an M.A. in the same subject from the University of North Carolina in Chapel Hill.

In 1977, he freelanced an editorial cartoon to the nearby *Durham Morning Herald*. Two years later, he became the *Herald's* first full-time editorial cartoonist, a position he held until 1988. He is now a freelance cartoonist, writer, and editor — when not serving as production manager for another Durham publication, *The Urban Hiker.*

Rogers has served as Secretary-Treasurer of the Association of American Editorial Cartoonists since 1998 and was editor of its quarterly magazine, *The Notebook,* from 1996 to 2002. He has written about editorial cartooning for a number of magazines. In December 2002 he chaired a nationally televised panel in Morristown, New Jersey, marking the 100th anniversary of the death of Thomas Nast.

In 2000, Rogers won the Association of Alternative Newsweeklies award for editorial cartooning. He is most proud, though, of the Ink Bottle Award he received from the AAEC in 1999 for longtime service to the Association.

V. Cullum Rogers
1002 Wells St.
Durham, NC 27707

First in Flight from Reality

[*Senator John Edwards decides not to seek re-election and runs for president instead.*]

Rob Rogers

From his college days in the heart of Oklahoma to his current staff position with the *Pittsburgh Post-Gazette,* Rob Rogers has been creating editorial cartoons with impact. His work is nationally syndicated by United Feature Syndicate, and regularly appear in *The New York Times, the Washington Post, USA Today, Newsweek* and a host of other papers. In 1994 Rogers' depiction of "The Gingrich Who Stole Christmas" graced the cover of *Newsweek's* year-end issue.

Born in Philadelphia, Rogers began copying his favorite characters out of the *Inquirer's* comics pages as soon as he was old enough to grasp a pencil. His interest in "political" cartooning was cultivated at Oklahoma State University, where he was asked to draw cartoons about student issues for the college paper. After graduating in 1984 from Carnegie-Mellon University in Pittsburgh with an MFA in painting, Rogers was hired as staff cartoonist by *The Pittsburgh Press.* When the *Press* was bought by the *Pittsburgh Post-Gazette* in January 1993, Rogers joined the new *Post-Gazette.*

Rogers received the 2000 Overseas Press Club Award, the 1995 National Headliner Award, and has won eight Golden Quill Awards. Rogers, who was a finalist for the Pulitzer Prize in 1999, aims to provoke: "If I beat someone over the head with an opinion, all they walk away with is a sore head. If I can make them laugh, I know I've reached them."

Rob Rogers
34 Blvd. of the Allies
Pittsburgh, PA 15222
rob@robrogers.com

John Rose, Jr.

John R. Rose, Jr. has always wanted to be a cartoonist. A native Virginian, Rose graduated from James Madison University in 1986 with a bachelor of fine arts degree in art and art history.

After graduation he drew freelance sports cartoons for newspapers in northern Virginia. He joined Byrd Newspapers of Virginia in 1988, starting at the *Warren Sentinel* in Front Royal, and then moving to the *Harrisonburg Daily News-Record*. His cartoons appear in other papers across Virginia and are distributed by the Scripps Howard News Service. His work has won awards from the National Newspaper Association and the Virginia Press Association.

In 1996, Pelican Publishing published a book of his editorial cartoons, "Cartoons That Fit the Bill: An Editorial Cartoon Collection About Washington and Beyond." He has also had cartoons featured in "Best Editorial Cartoons of the Year" annual collection.

Since 1998, Rose has worked on King Features' nationally syndicated comic strip "Barney Google and Snuffy Smith," first as an inking assistant to creator Fred Lasswell and then taking over all of the drawing responsibilities after Lasswell's death in March 2001.

Rose also creates Kids' Home Newspaper, a weekly childrens' cartoon/activity page that has been syndicated by Copley News Service since 1991. He has published six children's activity books, and his cartoon illustrations have also appeared in books from Scholastic and Magination Press.

He lives with his wife Karen and daughters Meredith and Sarah in Harrisonburg. When he's not cartooning, he enjoys spending time with his family, eating pizza and freshwater fishing.

John Rose, Jr.
95 Laurel St.
Harrisonburg, VA 22801
rosetoon@aol.com

Drew Rougier-Chapman

Drew Rougier-Chapman is a new cartoonist. He is not a particularly young cartoonist, just a new cartoonist. A lawyer by training, Rougier-Chapman (who publishes his work under the name of Drew Chapman) could no longer ignore the political jokes that kept popping up in his head whenever he read the newspaper. Realizing he had no artistic training or talent, Rougier-Chapman signed up for art classes, which he optimistically takes to this day.

His work can currently be seen online at CommentaryPage.com.

Drew Rougier-Chapman
133 North Wayne St.
Arlington, VA 22201
703-812-7882
rougierchapmana@yahoo.com
www.commentarypage.com

"NO DECISION HAS BEEN MADE..."

Steve Sack

Steve Sack has been the editorial cartoonist for the *Minneapolis Star Tribune* since 1981.

Sack began his newspaper career while attending the University of Minnesota, where he illustrated features and drew editorial cartoons for the school paper, *The Minnesota Daily.* Two years later he was hired as staff cartoonist for the *Journal-Gazette* in Fort Wayne, Indiana, and eventually returned to Minnesota three years after that to join the *Star Tribune.*

With partner Craig Macintosh he also produces the children's Sunday Comics feature "Professor Doodles."

Sack's editorial cartoons were recognized in 2004 by the Society of Professional Journalists with its Sigma Delta Chi award.

Sack resides in Bloomington, Minnesota, with his wife Beth and son Adam.

Steve Sack
sack@visi.com

NUCLEAR PROLIFERATION

WHAT IT SEEMS LIKE

Ben Sargent

A sixth-generation Texan, Ben Sargent was born in Amarillo in 1948 into a newspaper family. He learned the printing trade from age 12 and started working for the local daily as a proof runner at 14.

Sargent attended Amarillo College and received a bachelor of journalism degree from the University of Texas at Austin in 1970. He worked as a reporter for five years, covering the state capitol for *The Corpus Christi Caller-Times, Long News Service*, and United Press International. In 1974, he started drawing editorial cartoons for *The Austin American-Statesman.*

Sargent's cartoons are distributed nationally by Universal Press Syndicate, and have won numerous awards including the Free Press Association's Mencken Award in 1988. He was given Amarillo College's first "Distinguished Alumnus Award" in 1993, and has been a three-time finalist for the Pulitzer Prize, winning journalism's biggest award in 1982 for editorial cartooning.

Sargent served as president of the Association of American Editorial Cartoonists in 1988-1989, and is a founding director of the Austin Steam Train Association Inc. He is qualified as a steam-locomotive fireman, as well as a brakeman and conductor.

Sargent is married to Diane Holloway, the *American-Statesman* television critic. They have a daughter, Elizabeth, and a son, Sam.

Dave Sattler

Dave Sattler first applied for the job of editorial cartoonist for the *Lafayette Journal and Courier* in Indiana at the age of 19, when he was a student at Purdue University. The editor turned him down.

True to his tenaciousness, he stood in front of that same editor's desk a year later and convinced him to "give it a try" despite the fact that he wouldn't graduate from Purdue for another year. 35 years later, Sattler is still drawing cartoons for the *Lafayette Journal and Courier*.

Over the last three decades Sattler has published three collections of cartoons featuring comments on pivotal events of Lafayette, the state of Indiana and the nation. Sattler's work has been selected for inclusion in "Best Editorial Cartoons of the Year" 13 times from 1982 to 2002.

He received the Hoosier State Press Association Award for Best Editorial Cartoonist of 1996 and was runner-up in 2001. He gives frequent presentations for Purdue University on creative thinking.

Sattler serves as a director on many community boards including the Greater Lafayette Convention and Visitors, Indiana Vocational Technical College Development, United Way and Tippecanoe Arts Federation.

In addition to all his community involvement he is, foremost, a husband to his wife Nancy, devoted father to his four grown children and a doting grandfather.

EARLY EDUCATION...

Dave Sattler
Box 206, Lafayette, IN 47902
Dave@lafayetteprinting.com
www.sattlercartoons.com

Joe Sharpnack

Joseph Sharpnack is an Iowa City, Iowa, editorial cartoonist who currently produces cartoons under contract for the *Iowa City Gazette*.

His work appears in numerous national and international publications including *The Washington Post, the Sacramento Bee, Michigan Chronicle,* and *Liberal Opinion Week*. His cartoons have also appeared in *USA Today, Washington Post/Newsweek Interactive* and the *Financial Times*.

His awards include an honorable mention from the 2002 John Fischetti Cartoon Competition, and the 1991 Chicago Headliner Club's Peter Lisagor award. In 1989, he became the first college newspaper cartoonist to be nominated for the Menken Award.

He currently has several novelty flipbooks being distributed by Andrews McMeel publishing and has working to create two online comic strips for Tribune Media.

Sharpnack is the drummer for Oink Henderson and The Squealers, the eastern Iowa Rock & Roll sensation that is "not responsible for questionable performances, poor taste or paranormal aberrations at any time during the show."

His play, "Little Cheep-Cheep the Chicken" was rejected by New York play publishers, Samual French, Inc. ... The bastards.

Joe Sharpnack
301 E. Market St.
Iowa City, IA 52245
319-338-9609
joe@sharptoons.com
www.sharptoons.com

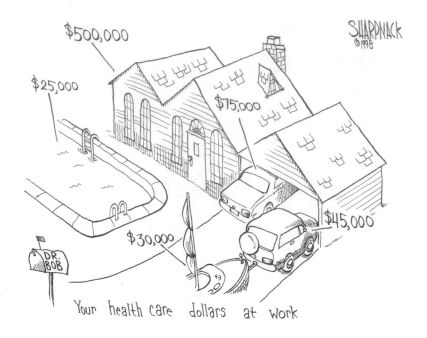

Your health care dollars at work

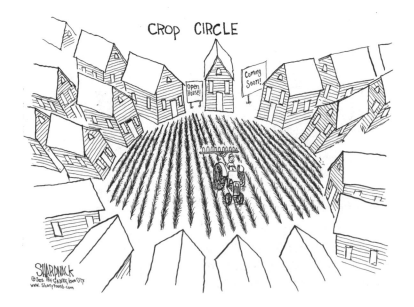

CHANNEL SURFING WITH RUPERT MURDOCH

Drew Sheneman

Drew Sheneman has been the editorial cartoonist at *The Star-Ledger* in Newark, New
Jersey, since graduating from Central
Michigan University in
1998 with a major in
fine art and a useless
minor in art history.

He's managed to
draw for New Jersey's
largest paper for over
five years now without
being fired. Prior to
joining the *Ledger,*
Drew interned as a cartoonist at *The Detroit
News* and *Oakland Press.*

His awards include the Charles Schulz
Award from Scripps Howard, The Deadline
Club Award from the New York Society of
Professional Journalists, and the John
Locher Award from the AAEC.

Sheneman is nationally and internationally
(if you count Canada) syndicated by Tribune
Media Services. He lives in Madison, New
Jersey, with his lovely wife of five years,
Tanna

Drew Sheneman
dsheneman@starledger.com

HUMAN SHIELD

Kevin Siers

Kevin Siers creates five cartoons a week for *The Charlotte Observer* in North Carolina. A native of Minnesota, he's been drawing for the *Observer* since 1987.

He began his career by drawing editorial cartoons for his hometown community newspaper between shifts working in the local iron-ore mines. While at the University of Minnesota, Siers joined the staff of the *Minnesota Daily* as editorial cartoonist, where his work won the John Locher Award and the Sigma Delta Chi Award from the Society of Professional Journalists.

His cartoons are distributed to over 400 newspapers nationwide by King Features Syndicate. They have also been published in *The New York Times*, *the Washington Post*, *Newsweek* and *USA Today*.

Kevin Siers and his wife and son reside in Charlotte.

Kevin Siers
P.O. Box 30308
Charlotte, NC 28230
704-358-5018
ksiers@charlotteobserver.com
www.charlotte.com

Mickey Siporin

Cartoonist, filmmaker and teacher, Mickey Siporin traces his interest in editorial cartooning and social issues to the regular political discussions he used to have with his father while growing up in Chicago in the 1950s.

His cartoons have appeared in the *Los Angeles Times, the New York Times, the Newark Star-Ledger, Toronto Star, Z Magazine, Funny Times* and *the Village Voice.*

In the 1970s he wrote "Spidey Super Stories" for the Children's Television Workshop version of Marvel Comics. His short comedy films have been shown on Cinemax, HBO, PBS, and Showtime. His parody of educational films, "How to Eat," is in the permanent collection of the Museum of Modern Art in New York City.

In 1995, Siporin won the New York Press Association's second-place award for editorial cartooning.

Mickey Siporin
www.mickeysiporin.com/
mickey@mickeysiporin.com

Mike Smith

Mike Smith was born in San Francisco in 1960 and spent the early years of his life living in a flat on the corner of Haight and Ashbury streets.

Smith knew he wanted to be a professional cartoonist when he saw how much trouble his cartoons stirred up when they appeared in his college newspaper, the *Los Angeles Loyolan*. After some advice from Paul Conrad at the *Los Angeles Times*, he began sending packages of his materials to newspapers in search of a job.

Smith first became fascinated with Las Vegas after seeing Francis Ford Coppola's ''One From The Heart.'' He sent his cartoons to the *Las Vegas Sun*, which started running his work when he was still a senior in college. The following year he won first place in the Chicago Tribune Syndicate's Campus Cartoon Contest, and late in 1983, after persistently pursuing a position, he was hired by the *Sun*.

His work is syndicated by King Features Syndicate and is frequently published in the *Los Angeles Times, Newsweek* and *the New York Times*. It has also appeared on MSNBC, ''CBS Sunday Morning'' and C-Span. He also draws an editorial cartoon each Thursday for *USA Today* and a weekly, nationally syndicated editorial cartoon on NASCAR Winston Cup stock car racing.

Smith has won several awards from the Nevada Press Association and has placed second for best editorial cartoons from the National Headliner Awards two years in a row. Casino owners, senators, celebrities, Bill Clinton and even the Pope have asked for originals of his work.

His wife Julie is an executive with U.S. Bank. They have two daughters, Morgan, 11, and Lexie, 9.

Mike Smith
2275 Corporate Circle Dr.
Henderson, NV 89074
702-259-4092
smith@vegas.com

Rob Smith, Jr.

Born in Orlando, Florida, Rob Smith, Jr. began drawing professionally at the age of 16, doing caricatures at local attractions and creating advertising art. After high school, he attended the Ringling School of Art in Sarasota, Florida; the Joe Kubert School of Cartoon and Graphic Art in Dover, New Jersey; and Rollins College in Winter Park, Florida.

During a stint drawing caricatures at Disney World, Smith joined the City of Orlando in 1985 as an artist and draftsman (hired by Jeff Parker, who is now editorial cartoonist with *Florida Today*). In 1992, he began creating editorial cartoons for the *Winter Park Observer*. Smith also regularly contributes cartoons to *The Ledger*, in Polk County, Florida.

Smith's editorial cartoons are syndicated by DBR Media and are featured every week on the web site of the nationally syndicated "Glenn Beck Radio Program."

One of Smith's favorite pastimes is volunteering as a motivational speaker on creativity and cartooning for schools and civic organizations. He also heads a professional/amateur cartoonists group in Tampa Bay, The Suncoast Inkslingers, and an Orlando group, The Central Florida Inkslingers.

Rob Smith, Jr.
robsmithjr@robsmithjr.com
www.robsmithjr.com

John Spencer

John Spencer joined the *Philadelphia Business Journal* as editorial cartoonist in 1985. His cartoons on national issues are self-syndicated to newspapers across the United States.

Spencer has won numerous awards, including first place for editorial cartooning from the Philadelphia Chapter of the Society of Professional Journalists in 1998, 1999 and 2002.

Born in 1959, he grew up in Ithaca, New York, and is a 1981 graduate of the State University College at Buffalo.

He and his wife Kathy live in Wynnewood, Pennsylvania, with their daughters Caroline and Jane. In his (increasingly spare) spare time, he enjoys collecting vintage guitars and playing them badly enough to guarantee himself plenty of time alone.

John Spencer
400 Market Street, Ste. 300
Philadelphia, PA 19106
215-238-5150
jspencer@bizjournals.com

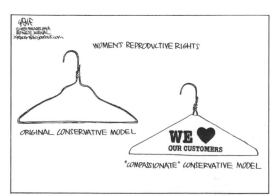

KERRY'S NEXT MOVE...   BUSH'S NEXT MOVE...

LET ME GUESS... YOU HAVE A KID ENTERING COLLEGE THIS FALL?

Jeff Stahler

Jeff Stahler has been an editorial cartoonist for *The Cincinnati Post* since 1985. His cartoons are nationally syndicated by United Media, and he's a weekly contributor to *USA Today* and "CNN Headline News."

Stahler's work is frequently reprinted in major publications including *Newsweek* and *The New York Times*. He has won numerous national and local awards. He is also the creator of "Moderately Confused," a whimsical slice-of-life daily comic panel appearing in over 300 newspapers world-wide.

A native of Bellefontaine, Ohio, Stahler graduated from the Columbus College of Art and Design in 1977 with a BFA. Before joining *The Cincinnati Post*, he was the editorial cartoonist with *The Columbus Citizen-Journal*.

He lives in Cincinnati, Ohio, with his wife Jeani and their children, Maggie and Alex.

Jeff Stahler
jstahler@cinci.rr.com

OH! WHAT A PERFECT GIFT... 'BABY'S FIRST SCHEDULE BOOK'!

CLINTON'S STRENGTH

CLINTON'S WEAKNESS

Scott Stantis

A San Diego, California, native, Scott Stantis has been the editorial cartoonist for Alabama's *The Birmingham News* since 1996. Copley News Service syndicates his work to over 400 newspapers. He is a weekly contributor to *USA Today*, and his cartoons have appeared in *Newsweek, the New York Times, the Chicago Tribune, Los Angeles Times*, and on "Nightline and "CBS This Morning."

He is also the creator of the comic strip "The Buckets," which is syndicated by United Features to over 100 newspapers.

Stantis previously held editorial cartoon positions at *The Commercial Appeal* in Memphis, Tennessee, and *The Arizona Republic* in Phoenix.

He has won or placed in numerous contests including the National Headliner, the Mencken Awards and Fischetti Awards. A collection of his editorial cartoons was published under the title "Taking a Stantis."

He is a former president of the Association of American Editorial Cartoonists. He currently has a seat on the Board of Directors of the Epilepsy Foundation of Central and Northern Alabama and the Spina Bifida Foundation of Alabama. He is also Chairman of the Industry Outreach Committee for the Herblock Fund of the AAEC.

Scott Stantis lives in Hoover, Alabama, with his wife of over two decades, Janien Fadich, and sons Spencer and Trevor, as well as his dog, Dogzilla.

THE BUSH PATROL HERE...RESISTANCE IS FUTILE!

CAN'T YOU CONTROL THIS THING A LITTLE BETTER?

Elena Steier

While pursuing her teacher certification, Elena Steier was informed by one of her students that she'd make a better cartoonist than a teacher. It turned out to be, as they say, a defining moment. She now works full time as a freelance cartoonist.

Currently, she concentrates most of her time on her self-published comic book, "The Vampire Bed and Breakfast," the story of a 350 year old vampire still living with his mom. The latest issue, "The Revenge of the Vampire Bed and Breakfast," is tantamount to a 64-page political cartoon (published thanks to a generous grant from the Xeric Foundation).

Steier and her husband Rod have four children. She has a comparative literature degree from Trinity college in Hartford, Connecticut. While the kids were growing up, Steier produced children's shows for West Hartford Public Access television and editorial cartoons for the local paper.

Today, Steier's political cartooning is confined to the web. Please visit her website at http://striporama.com. Not only is it political, it's free.

INFOTAINMENT

TWO RABBIS AND A PALESTINIAN WALK INTO A BAR...DETAILS AT SIX....

BLAM

CONVERSATIONS WITH VLAD

A SOUL SEARCHING EXCHANGE BETWEEN U.S. PRESIDENT GEORGE W. BUSH AND RUSSIAN PRESIDENT VLADIMIR PUTIN

SOMEDAY YOU WILL HAVE TO EXPLAIN TO ME HOW YOUR COUNTRY IS RALLYING BEHIND MONEY LAUNDERER PAVEL BORODIN.

AH, BORODIN, A FINE MAN WHO RUNS A BIG COMPANY.

I AM IN AWE OF MEN WHO MAKE GREAT BUNDLES OF CASH WITH MINIMAL EXPENDITURE OF TIME, ENERGY AND CAPITAL.

I HEAR YOU ARE SUCH A MAN YOURSELF. WE HAVE MUCH TO DISCUSS.

©2001 Elena Steier
West Hartford News 8-30-01

Ed Stein

Ed Stein has been the editorial cartoonist for the *Rocky Mountain News* in Denver, Colorado, since 1978. His cartoons are syndicated internationally to daily newspapers by United Media and have appeared in *The Washington Post, the New York Times, USA Today, Newsweek , U.S. News & World Report, Business Week, Playboy, People* and other publications.

In 1997 he began drawing "Denver Square," a six-day-a-week editorial comic strip about a fictional Denver family, named for a type of house common to the city.

Stein has won a number of awards for his cartooning, most recently in a special category of the 2001 John Fischetti Award for cartoons drawn after the World Trade Center attacks. He also has won the 1999 Scripps Howard Foundation National Journalism Award for Editorial Cartooning, the Dragonslayer Award, the World Hunger Media Award (for cartoons addressing the problems of world famine), and many awards from the Colorado Society of Professional Journalists Awards and Colorado Press Association Awards. He has been cited twice by the Best of the West Award, the Headliner Award, and the Robert F. Kennedy Award.

He is also a former president of the Association of American Editorial Cartoonists.

Ed Stein
100 Gene Amole Way
Denver, CO 80204
stein@rockymountainnews.com

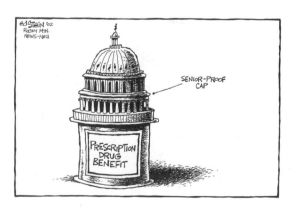

A la hora señalada...

Glenn "Marty" Stein

Glenn "Marty" Stein draws editorial cartoons for *La Prensa* in Orlando, Florida. He self-syndicates his work, along with his comic strip "El Oasis."

Stein was born in Miami on October 4, 1962. His interest in drawing began at a very early age, and although he drew some cartoons during his youth, most of his artwork depicted "serious" subjects like dinosaurs, ships and airplanes.

While attending the University of Florida, Stein became interested in editorial cartooning, and drew for *The Independent Florida Alligator.* He eventually appeared on the editorial page of *The Gainesville Sun* in 1986.

Stein also worked as an editorial cartoonist for *The Orlando Business Journal* and *The Apopka Chief.* In addition, he drew the comic strip "Mr. Tibs" for *Surf Ski* magazine of New South Wales, Australia, from 1989 to 1992.

Stein and his wife Marsha are raising their twin daughters, Aleah and Rebekah, in Apopka, Florida. Stein researches, writes and lectures on naval history and polar exploration.

Glenn "Marty" Stein
1268 Foxforrest Circle
Apopka, Florida 32712
407-884-4148
www.eloasis.tv
eloasis@earthlink.net

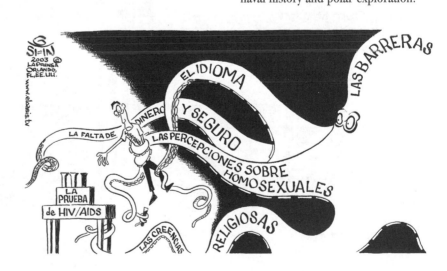

Tom Stiglich

Drawing cartoons is Tom Stiglich's life. Born and raised in Philadelphia, Pennsylvania, he has found cartooning to be a great way to

support a serious cheese steak addiction, and much more rewarding than rooting for the Phillies (one championship in 120 years).

Stiglich's first published cartoon appeared in the *Philadelphia Daily News* while he was attending Northeast Catholic High School. After completing high school he attended the Art Institute of Philadelphia, where graduated with honors in June 1988. Since then he has been an illustrator, art director and, for the past four years, a graphic designer at a weekly newspaper in Philadelphia.

Stiglich's editorial cartoons appear weekly in the *Northeast Times*, in Philadelphia, and in many New Jersey newspapers, including *The Haddon Herald, NEWSWeekly, The New Egypt Press, Community News, News Report, Plain Dealer* and *the Record-Breeze.*

His work has also been seen in *Newsweek*, in King Features Syndicate's "The New Breed," on greeting cards and in "Best Editorial Cartoons of the Year."

He enjoys reading, playing basketball, making fun of his friends and flossing his rather large teeth.

Tom Stiglich
TSTIG822@aol.com
www.tomstiglich.com

"THE CREW OF THE SHUTTLE COLUMBIA DID NOT RETURN SAFELY TO EARTH; YET WE CAN PRAY THAT ALL ARE SAFELY HOME." —GEORGE W. BUSH

Carlton Stoiber

Carl Stoiber is a freelance cartoonist, focusing on science, technology, the environment, arms control and non-proliferation.

Growing up in Boulder, Colorado, his first cartooning gig was a strip for his junior high school newspaper. "Twitterbird," his avian character, poked fun at teachers, adolescent crushes and jocks.

Stoiber received a B.A. (Summa Cum Laude, Phi Beta Kappa) and J.D. degrees at the University of Colorado and a degree in International Law at the University of London. He was a Rhodes Scholar at Oxford University, four years ahead of Bill Clinton.

Between 1969 and 1999, Stoiber held legal and policy positions in several federal agencies including the Departments of Justice and State, and the Nuclear Regulatory Commission. In the 1980s he cartooned for *State Magazine*. During his government career Stoiber was known for using cartoons to lighten up the atmosphere during heated negotiations. One memorable encounter occurred when President Reagan interrupted a highly-classified intelligence session with a surprise phone call to Stoiber about one of his cartoons.

Now out of government, Stoiber consults on international and nuclear law for multinational and U.S. government agencies and private organizations. His cartoons are regularly featured in *National Parks Magazine*, the National Academy of Sciences quarterly *Issues in Science and Technology* and *The Nonproliferation Review*, among other publications.

Carl Stoiber's wife Susanne has put up with him and his passion for high-altitude mountaineering since 1966.

Carlton Stoiber
2953 Arizona Ave., NW
Washington D.C. 20016
202-966-7793
crstoiber@earthlink.net

Sage Stossel

Sage Stossel does a weekly cartoon feature, "Sage, Ink," for *The Atlantic Monthly* web site. Her work has been featured by Cartoon Arts International/The New York Times Syndicate, *The Palm Beach Post*, *Nieman Reports*, *Editorial Humor*, and on CNN Headline News and elsewhere.

Stossel grew up in a suburb of Boston and attended Harvard University, where she majored in English and American Literature and Languages and did a weekly cartoon strip called "Jody," for the *Harvard Crimson*.

Aside from cartooning (which is her favorite part of her job) she is an editor of *The Atlantic* web site and an assistant editor for the print magazine. She lives in Cambridge, Massachusetts.

Sage Stossel
sstossel@theatlantic.com

"Drug Deal Going Bad"

Wayne Stroot

A former power lineman, Wayne Stroot's high voltage conservative cartoons have been electrifying his readers for more than a

decade. His work includes editorial cartoons, comic strips, advertisements, illustrations and caricatures.

Born and raised in St. Louis, Missouri, Stroot was bitten by the cartooning bug at

the age of 14. The following year, he saw his first published cartoon appear in Bell Telephone's trade magazine. His cartoons are now seen in over 50 newspapers across Nebraska, Kansas, Wyoming and South Dakota.

He has earned numerous awards for his editorial cartoons, including first place in National Newspaper Association Better Newspaper Contest in 2002 and 2003, and both first and second places in the 2001. He has also won four first place awards from the Kansas Press Association and two first place awards from the South Dakota Press Association.

Wayne Stroot
P.O. Box 788
908 W. 2nd St.
Hastings, NE 68902
402-461-1231
wstoons@inebraska.com

The Old Shell Game

Dana Summers

Dana Summers is a cartoonist at Florida's *Orlando Sentinel*. His work is syndicated nationally by Tribune Media Services and appears regularly in such publications as *The New York Times, the Washington Post, Time, Newsweek* and *Readers Digest*.

He is co-creator of the comic strip, "The Middletons," with fellow *Sentinel* cartoonist Ralph Dunagin, and is the creator of "Bound & Cagged," a comic strip seen in 150 papers nationally and internationally.

Born in Lawrence, Massachusetts, Summers is a graduate of the Art Institute of Boston and has attended the Massachusetts College of Art. He started cartooning during the 1970s, freelancing for weekly and college newspapers in Massachusetts. From l977 to 1980 he was a staff artist at the *Fayetteville Times* in North Carolina. Summers joined the *Orlando Sentinel* in May 1982, following two years in the same position with the *Dayton Journal Herald* in Ohio.

Among his honors are two Citation of Excellence from the Overseas Press Club, and three Sigma Delta Chi Southeast Awards from the Society of Professional Journalists.

Summers and his wife, Mary Jane, are the parents of three and live in Orlando, Florida.

Dana Summers
dsummers@orlandosentinel.com

THE "PARTIAL BIRTH ABORTION" BAN SIGNING CEREMONY

Ann Telnaes

Born in Sweden, Ann Telnaes attended the California Institute of the Arts and graduated with a Bachelor of Fine Arts degree, specializing in character animation. Before beginning her career as an editorial cartoonist, She worked for several years at Walt Disney Imagineering as a designer. She has also

been an animator for various studios in London, Los Angeles, New York and Taiwan.

Telnae's editorial cartoons have appeared in *The Washington Post, the Boston Globe, Le Monde, Courrier International, the Minneapolis Star Tribune, the Chicago Tribune, Los Angeles Times, Newsday* and *the New York Times*.

Her awards include the 2003 National Press Foundation's Berryman Award, the 2002 Maggie Award from Planned Parenthood, the 1997 National Headliner Award for editorial cartoons, and the 2001 Pulitzer Prize for editorial cartooning. In the spring of 2004, the Library of Congress published a book of her work.

Telnaes resides in Washington, D.C., with her husband, David Lloyd.

Ann Telnaes
www.anntelnaes.com

SADDAM TOPPLING NETWORK

Stephen Templeton

Stephen Templeton was born and raised in Lynchburg, Virginia. After graduating from The Art Institute of Pittsburgh and The School of Communication Arts, Templeton worked at *The Daily Progress* in Charlottesville, Virginia.

Since 1998, he has worked for *The Fayetteville Observer* in North Carolina as cartoonist and illustrator.

Templeton is married to his wife Christine, and has a step-son, Ryan, at the Virginia Military Institute.

Stephen Templeton
templets@fayettevillenc.com

Craig Mitchell Terry

Craig Mitchell Terry has been drawing local editorial cartoons for 25 years. He has been the Art Director for *Northwest Florida Daily News* for 13 years, and has won 20-some odd awards, including Gold and Silver ADDYS for illustration work.

Craig Mitchell Terry
850-863-1111
craigt@nwfdailynews.com

[Terry's take on Florida Gov. Jeb Bush.]

[Terry drew this after residents of a local island town went to great lengths to discourage visitors.]

Mike Thompson

Mike Thompson is editorial cartoonist for the *Detroit Free Press*. His work is syndicated to more than 400 publications via Copley News Service.

Thompson also draws for *USA Today* and has had his work reprinted in such publications as *Time, Newsweek, Forbes, the New York Times* and *the Wall Street Journal*. In addition, his cartoons have been featured on CNN, C-SPAN, the "NBC Today show," ESPN, CBS Sports and the Fox News Network.

Thompson began his career as contributing cartoonist for *The Milwaukee Journal* and later worked as staff cartoonist for the *St. Louis Sun* and the Copley Illinois newspapers before joining the *Free Press* in November of 1998.

His work has won numerous honors.

Mike Thompson
600 W. Fort St.
Detroit, MI 48226
313-222-6616
thompson@freepress.com

Tom Toles

Upon graduating from the State University of New York at Buffalo in 1973, Tom Toles went to work for the *Buffalo Courier-Express* after an editor there encouraged him to become the paper's full-time editorial cartoonist. He moved to *The Buffalo News* when the *Courier-Express* closed in 1982 and remained there until taking the late Herbert Block's position at *The Washington Post* in 2002.

When Toles moved southward to *The Post*, the self-proclaimed "liberal tempered with time" found himself living four blocks away from a "compassionate conservative" — and the Bush administration transformed from "policy abstraction … to neighbors."

Toles is syndicated by Universal Press Syndicate in over 200 newspapers. In 2002, he was named the editorial cartoonist of the year by *Editor & Publisher.* He has also received the John Fischetti Award, the Mencken Award, a Global Media Award for his environmental cartoons, and the 1990 Pulitzer Prize for editorial cartooning.

He, his wife and two children live in the Washington, D.C. area.

Tom Toles
1150 15th St., NW, Washington D.C. 20071

John Trever

John Trever has served as the editorial cartoonist at the *Albuquerque Journal* in New Mexico since 1976.

His work has been honored by the Society of Professional Journalists, the Free Press Association, the Overseas Press Club and the New Mexico Legislature. His cartoons are distributed to more than 350 daily papers by King Features Syndicate. They have been reprinted in a wide variety of magazines and books, have been collected in two volumes, amd may be seen on the World Wide Web.

The son of a college professor involved in the discovery of the Dead Sea Scrolls, Trever showed early interest in more contemporary publications by winning the first national Newspaper Comics Council contest at age 13 with a drawing of Pogo. He earned Phi Beta Kappa honors at Syracuse University, where he cartooned for the *Daily Orange,* and attended the University of Chicago on a polit-ical-science fellowship. He served with the Air Force in Wyoming as a Minuteman Launch Officer and worked as the staff artist and cartoonist for the Sentinel Newspapers in Denver before arriving in Albuquerque.

Trever and his wife Karen, a Montessori teacher, have five grown children. In his spare time he collects Lionel trains, enjoys bluegrass music and fantasizes that the Chicago Cubs will return to the World Series in his lifetime.

John Trever
jtrever@abqjournal.com

REDISTRICTING AND YOU

NOW PART OF THE 55TH HOUSE DISTRICT, JOE HACKNEY (D).

NOW PART OF 57TH HOUSE DISTRICT (INCLUDING KIDNEYS & SPLEEN) GORDON ALLEN (D).

STAYS IN 56TH HOUSE DISTRICT, VERLA INSKO (D).

NOW ATTACHED TO THE 32ND DISTRICT (GRANVILLE), JIM CRAWFORD.

J.P. Trostle (Jape)

During his career in publishing, J.P. Trostle has been an art director, illustrator, graphic designer, writer, editor and, last but not least, cartoonist. He is currently a page designer and illustrator for *The Herald-Sun* in Durham, North Carolina, where he also draws local editorial cartoons for a nearby sister publication, *The Chapel Hill Herald*.

After graduating in 1986 with a degree in Graphic Design from Indiana University of Pennsylvania (IUP), he drew caricatures at the boardwalk, worked as an animator and wrote material for the Teenage Mutant Ninja Turtles.

From 1992 to 1997, Trostle was editorial cartoonist for the *Sunday Patriot-News* in Harrisburg, Pennsylvania. His cartoons have appeared in "Best Editorial Cartoons of the Year," and are part of the permanent collection of the State Museum of Pennsylvania. His design work and illustrations have won multiple awards from both the Pennsylvania and North Carolina Press Associations.

He has designed and edited ten books on a variety of subjects, including two with Ted Rall about editorial cartoons: "Attitude" and "Attitude2." *[Seeing as full disclosure is all the rage these days, it should be noted I'm also the editor of this book.]*

For most of his career, Trostle has been signing his cartoons under the pen name "Jape," a nickname he's had since he was 6 — the same age, coincidentally, at which he decided he wanted to be a cartoonist. Only later did he discover it was, like, a real word.

He lives in Durham, North Carolina, with his wife Maura McLaughlin and a bevy of cats.

FIRST CLONED RAT MEETS FIRST CLONED CAT.

J.P. Trostle
jape@nc.rr.com

Gary Varvel

Since 1994, Gary Varvel — the editorial cartoonist for *The Indianapolis Star* — has been heckling politicians, prominent people and popular culture like an obnoxious fan at a ballgame.

Varvel was born in Indianapolis, Indiana, in 1957 and after college spent 16 years working as the chief artist for *The Indianapolis News.*

He is an eight-time winner of the Indiana Society of Professional Journalists' Award for Best Editorial Cartoon. Since 1995, he has won the award for Best Editorial Cartoonist in the Hoosier State Press Association Contest seven times.

Varvel's work is nationally syndicated through Creators Syndicate. His cartoons have appeared on CNN and in *Newsweek, the New York Times, USA Today, the Washington Times, National Review, World* magazine and *Sports Illustrated.*

He spends his afternoons as a part-time art teacher for Bethesda Christian School High School in Brownsburg, Indiana. Varvel is a member of Bethesda Baptist Church in Brownsburg and is a Sunday School Teacher for an adult class. He also serves on the Deacon board and Missions board.

Varvel lives in Brownsburg, Indiana, with his wife of 22 years, Carol. They have three children: Ashley, 19, Brett, 17, and Drew, 12.

Gary Varvel
gary.varvel@indystar.com

The Indianapolis Star; May 3, 2002

1981, PRESS-TELEGRAM

Dick Wallmeyer

Born in 1931 in Chicago, Illinois, Dick Wallmeyer attended the Chicago Academy of Fine Arts, and later served in the U.S. Air Force during the Korean War.

From 1961 to 1995, Wallmeyer was editorial cartoonist for the *Press-Telegram* in Long Beach, California, and has continued to freelance local cartoons to his former employer since "retiring."

His cartoons have appeared on CNN and in *The New York Times, the Washington Post, Time, Newsweek,* and *U.S. News & World Report.*

Wallmeyer's cartoons have been cited by the California Newspaper Publishers Association, and have won awards from the Greater Los Angeles Press Club three times. In 1963, his work won the National Safety Council Award.

From 1966 to 1973 his work was syndicated nationally through the Lew Little Syndicate and the Register and Tribune Syndicate.

When he is not drawing, Wallmeyer can be found out on the links playing golf.

1979, INDEPENDENT, PRESS-TELEGRAM

MARIJUANA FARMS

CALIFORNIA GOTHIC

2-01
PRESS-TELEGRAM

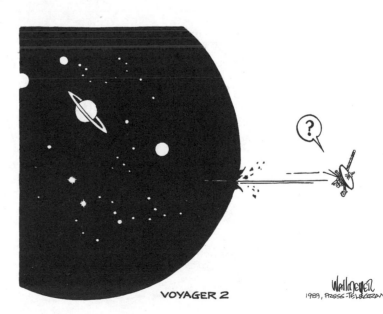

VOYAGER 2

1989, PRESS-TELEGRAM

Steve Wetzel

A graduate of Pennsylvania's Bloomsburg University with a degree in Special Education, Steve Wetzel works during the day in the field of mental retardation and is a trained mediator in special education. In the evening he works out of his home as a freelance cartoonist, drawing mainly for *The Patriot-News* in Harrisburg, Pennsylvania. His work has also appeared in the *Philadelphia Daily News,* and in numerous editions of "Best Editorial Cartoons of the Year."

Wetzel is also an avid *plein air* landscape artist and enjoys traveling to various locations in the eastern United States to capture the beauty of the landscape on his canvas.

He lives in the central Pennsylvania area with his wife Cathy. They have three children, Eddie, Stephanie, and Ben.

**Steve Wetzel
6155 Friar Rd.
Harrisburg, PA 17111
steve.wetzel2@gte.net**

[Left, Wetzel drew this cartoon after Penn State's Joe Paterno, the coach with the most wins in college football history, blamed his team's losing season on bad officiating — and the university's mascot (The Nittany Lion) lost a nationwide contest for the best mascot among college football fans.]

Signe Wilkinson

Signe Wilkinson is one of contemporary America's few women cartoonists. A native Philadelphian, Wilkinson began her career as a journalist for the *Daily Local News* in West Chester, Pennsylvania. She soon realized her interest in cartooning as she began drawing the subjects she was supposed to be covering. After attending the Pennsylvania Academy of the Fine Arts and freelancing, Wilkinson joined the staff of the *San Jose Mercury News.* In 1985 she returned to Philadelphia as a contributing artist at the *Philadelphia Daily News*.

From 1991 to the present, Wilkinson has deftly wielded her pen at local, national, and international politics. Though she examines a wide array of subjects, Wilkinson is best known for her insightful cartoons focusing on family and women's issues.

Wilkinson was the first woman to win the Pulitzer Prize for editorial cartooning in 1992, and served as the president of the Association of American Editorial Cartoonists in 1994–1995.

She contributes cartoons regularly to *Organic Gardening* magazine, the Institute for Research on Higher Education, and Oxygen.com.

Signe Wilkinson
wilkins@phillynews.com

Shrubbery©

Pam Winters

Pam Winters is a self-syndicated editorial cartoonist and artist from San Diego County, California. Her work appears in newspapers throughout California, as well as in *The Washington Post National Weekly Edition*.

Her first cartoon was published in the *North County Times* in 1998. From start to finish, Winters is the sole creator of each of her cartoons. Through her work, she strives to capture readers' attention and imagination, pushing them further in their thinking about today's issues. Social disparity, the erosion of the educational, justice and health care systems, political malaise, and integrity (and the lack thereof) are recurring themes in her work. The targets of her cartoons run the gamut and she does not play favorites. Nor is her work intended simply for laughs. These are serious drawings that make a statement, beginning a very gradual, yet powerful, process of influencing the hearts and minds of readers.

In addition to cartooning, Winters enjoys spending time with family, close friends and the kitties. She's also a music groupie in the extreme.

Pam Winters
pam@pamwinters.com
www.pamwinters.com

Monte Wolverton

Son of cartoonist Basil Wolverton, Monte Wolverton began his career in the early 1970s as a graphic designer. His cartoons and comics were first published in *CB Radio, Creative Computing, CAR-toons* and *Youth* magazines. He worked in advertising and publication design and illustration in Los Angeles, Seattle and Portland.

Wolverton's interests turned to editorial cartooning in the mid '90s, and his work is currently syndicated through caglecartoons.com.

He is also managing editor of *Plain Truth* magazine, an occasional contributor to *MAD* magazine and a board member of the Rat Terrier Club of America.

He resides with his wife Kayte in Westlake Village, California.

Monte Wolverton
monte@wolvertoon.com

Larry Wright

Larry Wright has been an editorial cartoonist at *The Detroit News* since 1976. He drew a comic strip, "Wright Angles," that was syndicated daily and

Sunday by United Features from 1976 to 1991, and currently draws the daily panel "Kit 'n' Carlyle," which has been in syndication by NEA Inc. since 1980.

In addition to the cartooning, he is an editor and associate creative director of *The Detroit News'* website, detnews.com. He is a past president of the AAEC and is webmaster of the AAEC website.

Wright lives in Canton, Michigan, with his wife of more than 40 years, Naoko. They have two children and four grandchildren.

The Detroit News
615 W. Lafayette
Detroit, MI 48226
lwright@detnews.com

Matt Wuerker

Matt Wuerker is a dedicated freelance cartoonist and illustrator. His op-ed illustrations are syndicated by the Los Angeles Times Syndicate and also by NewsArt.com.

His self-syndicated cartoons are widely published in all sorts of publications, ranging from *Funny Times, the Nation,* and *Z Magazine* to *the Washington Post, Los Angeles Times,* and *the Christian Science Monitor* (to name a few.) He's a regular contributor to Jim Hightower's "Lowdown" and TomPaine.com.

Two collections of his cartoons have been published: "Standing Tall in Deep Doo Doo, A Cartoon Chronicle of the Bush/Quayle Years," from Thunder's Mouth Press, and "Meanwhile in Other News, A Graphic Look at Politics in the Empire of Money, Sex and Scandal" from Common Courage Press.

He also co-authored 2003's "The Madness of King George" a collection of cartoons and essays on the "reign of George W. Bush."

Matt Wuerker
202-332-2846
mcwuerker@yahoo.com
www.mwuerker.com

Steve York

Steve York is the editorial cartoonist for *The Daily Journal* in Kankakee, Illinois. He also draws illustrations for the paper, and since 2001 has been producing a weekly local comic strip, "Captain Zero."

His editorial cartoons recently earned first place in the 2003 Illinois Press Association contest.

Born and raised in Hoopeston, Illinois (home of the Cornjerkers!), York was hired by the *Journal* in 1993, just a few months after graduating from Olivet Nazarene University in Bourbonnais, Illinois. He now lives in Bradley with his wife Jennifer, son Spencer, daughter Lydia and "Baby X," a third child due to arrive as this book goes to press.

When he's not cartooning, York spends most of his time with his kids, playing baseball in the backyard or bike riding around the neighborhood. He also teaches a senior high Sunday school class at Manteno Church of the Nazarene.

Steve is a huge Third Day fan and enjoys watching the silent comedy classics of Charlie Chaplin, Buster Keaton and Harold Lloyd. He dislikes writing biographical information about himself in the third person and eating anything involving coconut.

Steve York
syork@daily-journal.com

About Dork Storm Press

Founded in 1999, Dork Storm Press is the award-winning publisher of some of the most critically-acclaimed independent comic books and graphic novels published today.

Other titles from Dork Storm Press:
"Dork Covenant: The Collected Dork Tower, Volume I" — The first collection of the multiple Origins Award-winning comic book about a group of fanboys trying to make it in the real world. From Perky Goths to "Star Wars" fandom, Geek Chic has never been so sidesplitting. "Dork Tower may just be the perfect comic book," says Diamond Comics *Previews*. Available now: ISBN 1-930964-39-0; 160 pages, $15.99.

"Dork Tower: Global Village Idiot" — Irreverent internet mayhem is the rule of the day in the award-winning "Dork Tower" comic strip. A complete collection of the tech cartoons seen in *Interactive Week* and the *Chicago Sun-Times*. "One of the top Internet comics," says Tech TV. Available autumn 2004: ISBN 1-930964-68-4; 160 pages, $15.99.

"Snapdragons: The Kids are Alright" by John Kovalic and Liz Rathke — "SnapDragons" is the critically acclaimed comic adventures of a group of kids, the games they play and the power and magic of imagination. Meet the twins, Jake and Jody, and their gang as they transform their computer and role-playing games into priceless mayhem-filled misadventures. Available autumn 2004: ISBN 1-930964-52-8; 120 pages, $13.99.

"Chick Soup for the Super Soul: The Collected Dr. Blink, Volume 1" by John Kovalic and Christopher Jones — Who watches the watchmen (at reasonable hourly rates?) It's Dr. Blink: Superhero Shrink! From suicidal supermen who can't kill themselves (being invulnerable and all) to ex-childhood superstar superhero sidekicks trying to cope with the real world, Dr. Blink treats them all. Available spring 2005: ISBN 1-930964-63-3; 120 pages, $13.99.

Dork Storm Press
Box 45063 Madison, WI 53744
608-222-5522
sales@dorkstorm.com
www.dorkstorm.com

LINEA PERNICIOSA HABEBIMUS SEMPER *

About the AAEC

The Association of American Editorial Cartoonists is the world's largest organization of political cartoonists, with nearly 300 members in the United States, Canada and Mexico. Formed in 1957 by a small group of newspaper cartoonists led by John Stampone of the *Army Times*, the AAEC was created to promote and stimulate public interest in the editorial page cartoon and to create closer contact among political cartoonists.

The annual AAEC convention allows cartoonists and other association members — including publishers, writers, historians and collectors — the chance to meet face-to-face, talk shop and generally kvetch. Each year the gathering is held in a different North American city, usually in the summer, and consists of four days of panels, lectures, workshops, jam sessions and very, very late nights.

The AAEC has filed friend-of-the-court briefs in several cases dealing with freedom of the press, including the 1988 Supreme Court case *Flynt v. Falwell*. Aside from First Amendment issues, the Association does not take sides in political controversies.

The AAEC follows member artists and the industry through its quarterly magazine, *The Notebook*, and web site (http://www.editorialcartoonists.com). To apply for membership or obtain more information about the Association's activities, please visit the web site, send e-mail to wnicholson@nc.rr.com, or write to: AAEC, 1221 Stoneferry Lane, Raleigh, NC 27606.

CREDITS: Cover design by J.P. Trostle. Art on back cover, clockwise from upper left corner: Clay Bennett, John Cole, Mark Fiore, Mike Thompson, David Horsey, John Kovalic, Randy Bish, Joel Pett, Ann Telnaes, Kirk Anderson, Ted Rall, Dwane Powell, Kevin Siers, Tom Toles. Jet fighter, page 3: Mike Thompson. Senator Feingold, page 5: Jeff Stahler. AAEC logo by Karl Hubenthal.

* There will always be a deadline.